Snowdonia Slate Trail

Aled Owen

Rucksack Readers

Snowdonia Slate Trail

First published in 2018 by Rucksack Readers, 6 Old Church Lane, Edinburgh, EH15 3PX; reprinted with minor revisions in 2019.

Phone   0131 661 0262 (+44 131 661 0262)
Email: *info@rucsacs.com*
Website *www.rucsacs.com*

ISBN 978-1-898481-80-5

British Library cataloguing in publication data: a catalogue record for this book is available from the British Library.

Designed in Scotland by Ian Clydesdale: *www.workhorse.scot*

Printed and bound by Pario Print, Kraków, Poland

The mapping in this book is © Rucksack Readers, commissioned from Lovell Johns Ltd: *www.lovelljohns.com*. The mapping contains Ordnance Survey data © Crown copyright and database right 2018.

Publisher's note

All information was checked prior to publication. However, changes are inevitable: take local advice and look out for waymarkers and other signage e.g. for diversions. Before setting out, check the official website for updates and advice: *www.snowdoniaslatetrail.org*

Parts of the Trail may be wet underfoot, others are exposed and remote, and the weather in Wales is unpredictable year-round. You are responsible for your own safety, and for ensuring that your clothing, food and equipment are suited to your needs. The publisher cannot accept any liability for any ill-health, accident or loss arising directly or indirectly from reading this book.

Feedback is welcome and will be rewarded: email *info@rucsacs.com*

We are grateful to readers for their comments and suggestions on our first edition. All feedback will be followed up, and readers whose comments lead to changes will be entitled to claim a free copy of our next edition upon publication. Please email us at *info@rucsacs.com*.

Contents

Foreword/Rhagair *Crag Jones*   4

1 Planning to walk the Trail   5

Welsh language and pronunciation   8

Best time of year and weather   8

How long will it take?   9

Getting there and away   10

Accommodation and refreshments   11

Navigation, waymarkers and safety   12

Gradients and terrain   13

The Countryside Code and dogs   14

Packing checklist   16

2 Background information

2·1 The slate industry   17

2·2 Geology of Snowdonia   20

2·3 Snowdon   22

2·4 The Great Little Trains of Wales   24

2·5 Habitats and wildlife   27

3 The Way in detail

3·1 Bangor to Bethesda   31

3·2 Bethesda to Llanberis   35

3·3 Llanberis to Beddgelert   40

3·4 Beddgelert to Llan Ffestiniog   49

3·5 Llan Ffestiniog to Penmachno   57

3·6 Penmachno to Capel Curig   65

3·7 Capel Curig to Bethesda   71

4 Reference

Trail support, accommodation, maps and reading   74

Weather, glossary and credits   75

Index   76

Foreword

There lies ahead a journey from the depths of the earth through the crown of Wales. This beautiful book will lead you along secret paths to special places. You will experience an inspiring, fresh perspective on Snowdonia. As you trek through this region, you cannot fail to marvel at the sheer scale of the industry, the landscape, its people and their history. From sea to summit and back, enjoy the best of Wales from past to present.

Caradoc 'Crag' Jones, first Welshman to summit Everest

Rhagair

Naill fod yn eich cynefin neu o gymdogaeth arall, mae taith o'ch blaen o grombil y ddaear o amgylch copa Cymru. Bydd y llyfr prydferth hwn yn eich arwain ar lwybrau dirgel i lefydd cudd. Cewch gyfle i ymweld trwy ffordd newydd ar agwedd hollol wahanol o Eryri. Wrth gerdded yr ardaloedd hyn cewch argraff i waelod eich enaid o'r pur anfadrwydd, yr ysgelerder o'r gwaith, y dirwedd, ei bobol a'i hanes. O'r môr i'r mynydd a nôl, byddwch wedi profi'r gore o Gymru, o'r gorffennol hyd at heddiw, wrth eich nerthu am y dyfodol.

Bethesda and the Carnedd range

1 Planning to walk the Trail

Snowdonia is Wales' premier National Park, located in the north-west corner of the country. Historically it was the centre of the slate industry and an engine for growth during the industrial revolution. The 83-mile (134 km) long Snowdonia Slate Trail is a fully waymarked route which explores the Park's beauty and its context of slate heritage and culture. The Trail starts at Bangor and ends in Bethesda in the Ogwen valley, the home of the slate industry's Great Strike (1900 – 1903): see page 18.

The Trail is the culmination of four years of work by the voluntary Cwm Community Action Group, from the remote Snowdonia village of Cwm Penmachno. Once a slate village with some 500 residents, it is now a quiet backwater of about 70 people. The Group developed the Trail in order to stimulate business opportunities in the former slate villages while bringing this rich and important slate heritage to a wider audience.

The Trail is shaped like a leaf hanging from a stem. The stem takes you from Port Penrhyn on the outskirts of Bangor to Bethesda. From there, the Trail crosses moors and valleys, and follows rivers, gorges and forest tracks, in an anticlockwise circuit back to Bethesda. (If you prefer to walk the Trail clockwise, you will have to reverse the book's directions and sequence.)

This Trail was launched only in late 2017 and facilities are developing as its popularity grows. When planning your walk, give attention to planning transport, accommodation and refreshments.

Each of the suggested day sections described in this book ends at a village where bed and breakfast accommodation is available, at least if booked far enough ahead.

If you aren't experienced at long-distance walking, you may wish to download our *Notes for novices*: see page 75. We offer advice on appropriate gear, likely walking speeds and preparation.

Before you set out to complete the Trail, make sure that you are capable of several day-long walks on consecutive days, carrying whatever load you are likely to need in the conditions that you expect. Consider whether you need any support with travel or baggage.

Long-distance walks can be completed alone, and some people prefer the solitude and closeness to wildlife of this approach. Others, especially novices, will prefer the sociability and safety of walking with at least one companion. A lone walker certainly needs to have thought through how to handle problems in any kind of emergency, and to ensure that somebody knows his or her planned itinerary. That is important not only in case of accident or emergency, but also to avoid needless anxiety or even a wasted callout. Be aware that mobile coverage can be patchy in Snowdonia.

Table 1 Distances and stages

		miles	km	pages
	Bangor			
3·1		6·3	10·2	31-34
	Bethesda			
3·2		7·2	11·6	35-39
	Llanberis			
3·3		20·0	32·2	40-48
	Beddgelert			
3·4		14·4	23·2	49-56
	Llan Ffestiniog			
3·5		13·2	21·3	57-64
	Penmacho			
3·6		11·2	18·1	65-70
	Capel Curig			
3·7		11·0	17·6	71-73
	Bethesda			
Totals		*83·4*	*134·2*	

Tryfan and the Glyder range framing Llyn Ogwen

Welsh language and pronunciation

The Trail passes through some of the most Welsh-speaking areas of Wales. Although many signs are bilingual, often place names are not. Throughout this book we name lakes and rivers by their local, Welsh names, such as Llyn Padarn and Afon Ogwen (rather than Lake Padarn or River Ogwen). A short glossary of Welsh terms with their pronunciation is included on page 75.

Best time of year and weather

There is no single best time to walk the Trail: different seasons have different moods, lighting, vegetation and wildlife. An early spring or late autumn walk may offer better weather than one carried out in high summer. Winter weather is, on average, more likely to be dull, wet and cold than summer, but there is no certainty about any particular week. Overall, here are some factors to think about:

- Winter days are short, with only 7–9 hours of daylight between November and January; this constrains whether and how you can complete the Trail safely.
- Parts of Snowdonia are relatively undeveloped and many of its facilities (including some B&Bs) are closed in winter.
- Public transport, particularly the Snowdon Sherpa bus, is less frequent in winter.
- In high season, particularly over Bank Holidays, accommodation in some parts of the Trail may be busy.
- Midges and mosquitos are not a major issue, but if you decide to camp near water in summer, you may find them annoying.

Snowdonia, like any other range of western hills, has weather that is fast-changing and unpredictable. Often, as you pass from one valley to the next, you will experience a change in weather and micro-climate. So, as many walkers already know, you will need to be prepared for all weather: bring both sun cream and waterproofs! Weather forecasts can be obtained from the sources shown on page 74.

Rhiwbach quarry

How long will it take?

Table 2 Daily distances for various options from six to eight days

	6-day		7-day option A		7-day option B		8-day	
	miles	km	miles	km	miles	km	miles	km
Bangor 🏠▲								
							6·3	10·2
Bethesda 🏠▲	13·5	21·8	13·5	21·8	13·5	21·8	7·2	11·6
Llanberis 🏠▲△🚐	20·0	32·2	14·8	23·8	9·7	15·6	9·7	15·6
Nantlle ▲△🚐			5·2	8·4	10·3	16·6	10·3	16·6
Rhyd Ddu 🏠▲△🚐								
Beddgelert 🏠△🚐	14·4	23·2	14·4	23·2	14·4	23·2	14·4	23·2
Llan Ffestiniog 🏠▲	13·2	21·3	13·2	21·3	13·2	21·3	13·2	21·3
Penmachno 🏠▲	11·2	18·1	11·2	18·1	11·2	18·1	11·2	18·1
Capel Curig 🏠▲△🚐	11·0	17·6	11·0	17·6	11·0	17·6	11·0	17·6
Bethesda 🏠▲ (+bus to Bangor)								

🏠 B&B/hotel   ▲ hostel/bunkhouse   △🚐 campsite

Most people find they can complete the Trail comfortably inside seven walking days. Table 2 shows four options, albeit all are identical from Beddgelert onward. You can vary these further, to suit your preference for accommodation. In particular, the 20 miles from Llanberis to Beddgelert can be split if you are camping or book accommodation in the Nantlle valley, Y Fron or Rhyd Ddu. See pages 11-12 for accommodation suggestions.

Alternatively, you may decide to spend longer in one of the larger villages to visit some of their attractions. An extra day in Llanberis would give you time to climb Snowdon or to visit the National Slate Museum and Electric Mountain, which takes you on an underground tour of the pumped storage hydro-electricity station. A stay in Blaenau Ffestiniog (3·5 miles north of Llan Ffestiniog) would allow you a ride on the famous Ffestiniog Railway or a tour of the fascinating Llechwedd Slate Caverns.

Part 3 describes the Trail in seven sections, but most of these can be divided into sub-sections to allow you to vary the number of days and the length of each day's walk. Upon completion of the Trail, you can use the regular public transport back from Bethesda to Bangor. However, if you decide to walk the Trail as a series of one- or two-day walks, careful planning is needed to make your sections fit in with your transport arrangements. Public transport in some sections is poor, and two cars may be necessary.

A further option is to return to Bangor on foot after completing the Trail, made more interesting if you take a different route. From Bethesda, follow the Lôn Las Ogwen cycleway to return to the start. However, if arriving by car, be aware that secure car parking may be an issue.

Bed and breakfast accommodation is available in all villages at the end of each section. There is also a sprinkling of campsites and camping barns along the Trail which can widen your options. Wherever you plan to stay, book your accommodation well in advance.

When planning your walk, be realistic about likely walking speed. In practice, few walkers sustain more than 2-2·5 mph (3·2-4 kph) over a full day of walking, though for short sections it is easier to keep up a faster pace. Many factors can slow you down, including the size of your group, the nature of the terrain, what weight you are carrying, the amount of altitude gain/loss, the number of stiles and other obstacles and how often you stop for breaks.

Getting there and away

Bangor is easily accessible by car and train, being on the main A55 North Wales Coast Road and also on the London to Holyhead mainline railway. The journey times shown in Table 3 are the shortest identified in 2017. Car journey times are based on average speeds with no allowance for traffic delay or stops.

The nearest major airports are Liverpool and Manchester, where you can catch the train or rent a car. However, hiring your rental car for a week can be expensive and secure parking may be problematic. Unless there is a non-walking driver in your company, you are likely to find that the car is never in the right place.

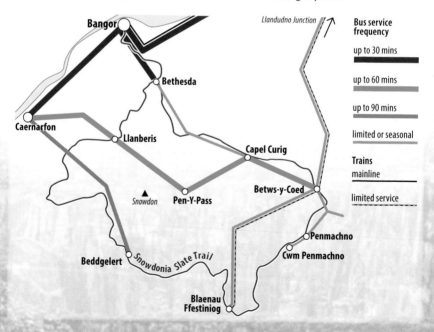

Table 3 **Distances and shortest journey time from selected places to Bangor**

	miles	km	by bus	by train	by car
Holyhead	25	40	1h 20m	25m	30m
Chester	63	101	4h 15m	1h 5m	1h 15m
Manchester	99	159	5h 15m	2h 15m	2h
Birmingham	143	230	6h 10m	3h 15m	2h 45m
London	255	410	9h 35m	3h 10m	5h
Glasgow	299	481	10h 25m	5h 20m	5h

All figures are rough guidelines only: for sources, see page 74.
Check timetables carefully in advance; winter timetables usually differ from summer.

Those who decide to walk the Trail in several expeditions may find themselves having to rely on a car. However, getting back to your car can be a lengthy journey by public transport and a second car, although not so ecologically friendly, may be the sensible choice in some instances. Bus services are limited in certain parts of the Trail: see page 74 for sources.

Accommodation and refreshments

Where you stay will depend on how many days you want to spend on the walk. Some places have many sights and attractions worth exploring, or you may prefer to return to visit them after your walk is completed. The layout of this book suggests you book accommodation in Bangor, perhaps Bethesda, Llanberis, Beddgelert, Llan Ffestiniog, Penmachno, Capel Curig and finally, after catching a bus from Bethesda, in Bangor – unless needing to complete your homeward travel immediately. Details were correct when we went to press, but check carefully for updates.

Table 4 **Accommodation and refreshments**

	miles from last place	km from last place	B&B/ hotel	hostel/ bunkhouse	campsite	pub/ café	food shop/ takeaway
Bangor			✓	✓		✓	✓
Bethesda	6·3	10·2	✓🛈	✓		✓	✓
Llanberis	7·2	11·6	✓	✓▲	✓	✓	✓
Waunfawr	3·8	6·1			✓	✓🕒	
Y Fron	4·2	6·8		✓		✓🕒	✓
Nantlle	1·7	2·7	✓		✓		
Rhyd Ddu	5·1	8·2	✓	✓	✓	✓	
Beddgelert	5·2	8·4	✓		✓	✓	✓
Croesor	4·4	7·2				✓🕒	
Tanygrisiau	4·6	7·4	✓			✓	
Blaenau Ffestiniog	1·9	2·9	✓	✓		✓	✓
Llan Ffestiniog	3·5	5·7	✓	✓		✓	✓
Penmachno	13·2	21·3	✓	✓		✓	
Conwy Falls	2·8	4·6				✓	
Betws-y-Coed	2·5	4·0	✓	✓	✓	✓	✓
Capel Curig	5·9	9·5	✓	✓	✓	✓	✓
Bethesda	11·0	17·6	✓🛈			✓	✓

🛈 *Accommodation in Bethesda is limited and some is distant from the Trail.* 🕒 *limited opening hours.*
▲ *Lodge Dinorwig is a few miles short of Llanberis, directly on the route, and provides food and bunkhouse accommodation.*

Some locations, such as Llan Ffestiniog and Penmachno, have limited accommodation, and it's essential to book these well in advance. Lodge Dinorwig is next to the route and provides food and bunkhouse accommodation. Y Fron Development Group is developing a luxury bunkhouse a few miles north of Nantlle, again directly on the route. Trigonos in Nantlle provides bed and breakfast if not booked out by groups, and Tal -y-Mignedd farm has a campsite and one caravan. Overnighting at these locations would allow you to divide the section from Llanberis to Beddgelert into two days. Idwal Cottage YHA and Snowdonia Mountain Lodge are located 2 and 3 miles south of Bethesda respectively. They enjoy fantastic surroundings.

Most land within Snowdonia National Park is privately owned and has specific uses, such as farming (mostly for sheep and cattle) or forestry. Wild camping is not allowed unless permission is specifically granted by the respective landowner or farmer. This is also the case in any unfenced and isolated upland areas. The access land provisions of the Countryside and Rights Of Way Act (CROW) specifically state that wild camping is forbidden unless permission is granted.

Note that the 13·2-mile section between Llan Ffestiniog and Penmachno is both rugged and remote. There is nowhere en route for refreshments, so before setting off you should buy and carry all the food and drink you need.

Although this is a new Trail, a number of local companies have already undertaken to provide walkers with a variety of services such as baggage handling and local transport. Some of these operators may help you to solve any logistic problems in your arrangements: see page 74.

Navigation, waymarkers and safety

The Snowdonia Slate Trail has been developed since 2013, and has benefitted from the advice and input of Snowdonia National Park, Conwy and Gwynedd County Councils and The Ramblers. As a result, the waymarking has been designed to be sufficient for navigational purposes while minimising clutter and avoiding any negative impact.

The waymarkers, mostly fixed to existing posts, are concentrated at junctions and areas of potential confusion. The effectiveness of the waymarking locations has been trialled on the ground but walkers of the Trail should carry, and be able to use, an appropriate map and compass so they are able to re-orientate themselves if necessary. If you haven't seen a waymarker for 20 minutes or so, consider the possibility that you are off-route – unless on a very clear track where waymarkers will be sparse because there is no room for doubt. Examples include the drove road into Croesor, the rising track from Capel Curig to Llyn Ogwen and the Trail through Beddgelert forest. If you have strayed offroute, it is usually easier to backtrack to the last waymarker you saw than to try to recover from a missed turning by carrying on regardless.

Various other resources are available from the official website, including down-loadable brochures, and a mobile app: see **www.snowdoniaslatetrail.org**.

The route includes some minor roads and walkers should always be aware of other road users, including bicycles on cycleways. In poor visibility, try to wear clothes that make you easily seen by vehicle drivers. Although it is usually safer to walk on the right hand side of the road, to face oncoming traffic, there are places where you should take to the left hand side temporarily, to improve sight lines – for example parts of the stretch from Penmachno Mill to Conwy Falls.

The Trail visits some fairly remote places, and, as for all hilly or exposed walking, your welfare depends on maintaining body warmth and hydration whatever the weather. Getting lost or injured can have serious consequences, especially if you walk alone. Do not assume that your mobile phone will have a signal. Although mobiles (cellphones) have their uses for making arrangements, never rely on your mobile in an emergency. For a summary of the Mountain Code and how to deal with emergencies in the mountains, see page 23.

Gradients and terrain

The Trail follows established public rights of way and permissive paths, and is generally of easy to moderate gradient. However, there are some areas of steeper ascent out of the valleys, in particular on the Pilgrims' Way out of Waunfawr, into the forestry above Rhyd Ddu, sections in the mountains above Croesor and climbing out of the upper Cynfal valley. However, these climbs are not too long or difficult, and the average hill walker will find no surprises. This Trail is easier than, for example, many of the National Trails of England and Wales. However, the walker should be prepared for a number of consecutive long days over paths which are generally unimproved. Rough, faint and wet moorland paths can make for strenuous walking. If you opt to climb Snowdon, you can expect more dramatic altitude gains, but even this depends on which summit route you choose: see pages 22-3. The diagram on our inside back cover shows an altitude profile of the Trail.

The Trail passes through varied terrain, following minor roads and lanes, paved and unpaved cycleways (former railway trackbeds), forest tracks, and paths across fields, moorland and hillsides. The route has been designed to avoid bogs where possible, but walkers need to take great care to avoid wet feet on the Migneint moors.

It is possible to stay dry, even in winter, if you identify and pass around the marshy areas. Some of these sections are remote, and walkers should be very aware of this, especially during bad weather. Those new to long-distance walking should consult our *Notes for novices*: see page 75.

The Trail has been developed by a community group with limited resources and most paths remain unimproved, maintaining a feeling of wildness. The route follows wild tracks through remote areas, and at present there are no plans to increase accessibility by replacing them. There are many stiles on the route, including some fine and ancient examples – one in slate and two made of iron – part of the unique character of the area.

However, certain stretches of the route have been designed especially for wheelchair access, such as the riverside walk in Betws-y-Coed. Others can be used by people with robust wheelchairs, such as Lôn Las Ogwen cycleway, the lane along the Nant Ffrancon valley (with care - part of this is very steep) and the multi-use path from Rhyd Ddu to Beddgelert (Lôn Gwyrfai).

The Countryside Code and dogs

Natural England's official advice (which applies to all parts of the countryside in England and Wales) is given in its Countryside Code: see panel on page 15.

While developing this Trail, over 70 landowners and agencies were consulted, and agreement reached on the route and the waymarking. Please help us to maintain

Sheep graze beneath Moel Siabod

their goodwill by respecting their property: keep to footpaths, use the stiles, leave gates as you find them and take your litter home.

The countryside provides both home and work for local people. In this area, farming is the main activity, especially sheep farming. On the higher ground, March and April are the busiest months for lambing, which may continue into May. Never disturb pregnant ewes, nor approach young lambs which may afterwards be abandoned by their mothers.

The Trail passes through sheep farming areas for most of the way, so dog owners should think long and hard before deciding to bring even a well-behaved dog on this Trail. Dogs must always be kept under close control, especially anywhere near sheep, cattle and horses. Dogs must be kept well away from livestock which may be pregnant or have young. On Open Access land, dogs must be kept on a short lead between 1 March and 31 July to help protect ground-nesting birds, and all year round near farm animals. A farmer may shoot a dog which is attacking or chasing farm animals without being liable to compensate the dog's owner.

Also be aware that animals can occasionally pose a risk to walkers with dogs. If you are being chased or threatened by cattle or horses, let your dog off the lead so it can run away. Do not try to protect the dog: you will put yourself at risk. As soon as you let go of the dog, escape the field as quickly as you can. Walkers with any experience of livestock will avoid such emergencies by closely watching the animals' body language in order to anticipate what action to take.

The accommodation along the Trail comprises a mix of B&Bs, bunkhouses and campsites. If you plan to take your dog, you will have to seek out dog-friendly accommodation and eateries in suitable locations. You should always clean up after your dog if it makes a mess on the Trail, and dispose of the bag responsibly.

In addition, some areas through which the Trail passes are designated as Sites of Special Scientific Interest or Special Areas of Conservation and are protected by law to conserve features such as geology and habitats, including ancient woodlands, nesting birds and a host of other wildlife. Please respect these fragile areas.

Packing checklist

This list separates essential and desirable items. Gaiters are great for keeping boots and trousers dry and mud-free, and for protection from nettles and bushes where ticks may lurk. If you haven't worn your waterproof trousers recently, test them before you go, when there's still time to re-proof, mend or replace them. Protection from the sun is also important: take both hat and sunscreen.

Essential

- rucksack
- waterproof rucksack cover or liner(s)
- comfortable, waterproof walking boots
- specialist walking socks
- waterproof jacket and overtrousers
- clothing in layers (tops, trousers, jacket)
- gaiters
- hat (for warmth and/or sun protection)
- guidebook and compass
- water carrier and plenty of water (or purification tablets)
- enough food to last between supply points
- first aid kit, including blister treatment
- toilet tissue (preferably biodegradable)
- personal toiletries
- insect repellent and sun protection
- cash and cards; there are cash machines at Bangor, Bethesda, Llanberis, Beddgelert, Blaenau Ffestiniog and Betws-y-Coed.

Desirable

- walking poles
- whistle and torch: *essential* if you are walking alone or in winter
- plenty of spare socks
- gloves
- camera
- plenty of spare batteries and memory cards for camera
- binoculars – useful for watching wildlife
- notebook and pen
- pouch or secure pockets for keeping small items handy and safe
- mobile phone.

> Mobile phone coverage can be patchy and varies according to your network. Never rely on a mobile for personal safety.

Camping

If you are camping, you need more gear, including tent, groundsheet, sleeping mat and a warm sleeping bag. You may also want a camping stove, fuel, cooking utensils and food. Your rucksack will have to be much larger and heavier, with a capacity of about 50-80 litres. Camping could add about 10 kg to the weight of your rucksack: previous experience is advisable.

Typical slate fence

Vivian quarry, Llanberis

Along the Trail, you will see many examples of slate, which has been used in construction in Snowdonia since Roman times. In some villages, cottage walls, roofs and field fences are built almost entirely of slate. The fort at Segontium (Caernarfon) built in AD 77, was roofed in slate as was Conwy Castle (13th century).

By the end of the 1800s, Penrhyn was the largest slate quarry in the world; about 1 mile (1·6 km) long and 1,200 feet (370 m) deep. In its heyday, it employed nearly 3000 quarrymen. The industry now employs only a few hundred people. To keep the industry alive, companies are diversifying their products.

In the past, slate has been used for snooker tables, beds (like one made for Queen Victoria for her stay at Penrhyn Castle in 1859), lintels, fences, gravestones, whetstones and blackboards. Much slate now goes into road construction, whilst slate powder is used in cosmetics and toothpaste. Gardeners and architects use slate for decorative surfacing and features.

The Trail passes through many villages surrounded by tips of slate waste. Most of these quarries are now disused, with serious production only at Penrhyn (Bethesda), Llechwedd (Blaenau Ffestiniog) and Cwt y Bugail (near Cwm Penmachno). One might see these tips as sad blots on the landscape. However, slate is an integral part of the landscape and culture of this area of Wales.

Rhosydd mine

Lord Penrhyn, Penrhyn quarry and Bethesda

On inheriting the slate areas around Bethesda in 1781, Richard Pennant took over an arrangement whereby slate workers quarried plots of land under a 21-year lease system, avoiding the need to pay royalties to the landowner. In 1782, Pennant bought out the leases and offered employment to the slate workers, an action which created the foundation for the industrialisation of slate extraction and processing. By the 1790s, Pennant, now Baron Penrhyn, had expanded his property, sometimes legitimately but, in some cases perhaps illegally, giving rise to the local saying 'Steal a sheep, they hang you; steal a mountain, they make you a lord'.

The estate eventually came to George Sholto Gordon Douglas-Pennant (1836-1907) who became the ruthless owner of Penrhyn Slate quarry in Bethesda. His dealings with the quarrymen culminated in the 1900-1903 strike, the longest industrial dispute in British history at the time. The quarrymen ultimately gave up in the face of hunger and poverty, but the strike became an international political issue highlighting the conflict between the power of the landowner and the growing trade union movement.

This dispute changed the life of the slate villages of Wales. The advent of cheap foreign slate and clay or asbestos roofing tiles drastically reduced demand, while World War 1 took away many of the skilled workers. The industry never recovered.

Blaenau Ffestiniog: a village reinvented

The village is dominated by tips of slate waste and perhaps the perception that they are so unlovely resulted in Blaenau Ffestiniog's omission from Snowdonia National Park. Many feel that this action was short-sighted, and that the cascades of blue rock should be celebrated.

The area was not always associated with the surrounding tips. It is hard to believe that in 1756, Lord Lyttleton wrote 'If you have a mind to live long, and renew your youth, come and settle in Ffestiniog. Not long ago, there died in this neighbourhood an honest farmer who was 105 years of age. By his first wife he had 30 children, 10 by his second, 4 by his third and 7 by two concubines. His eldest son was 81 years older than his youngest and 800 of his descendants attended his funeral.' Such a reputation for longevity did not last as quarrying grew exponentially in the Victorian period, and diseases such as silicosis and pulmonary fibrosis took their toll.

Blaenau Ffestiniog

Llechwedd Slate Caverns

Llechwedd slate mine has long been operated by the Greaves family and became one of the most innovative in the industry. At first, its slate was exported using the Ffestiniog Railway. Blaenau rose to become a leading international supplier of slate after securing the contract to supply slates to Hamburg. A disastrous fire in 1842 destroyed many of Hamburg's public buildings and made 20,000 people homeless. Reconstruction took nearly 40 years, and most of the roofs were restored with slate from Llechwedd. Nowadays, the mine is a major tourist attraction with tramway rides deep into the mountain and a self-guided, audio-assisted walk through caverns and passages past displays of light and music.

Blaenau Ffestiniog has fewer than 5000 residents but, through community initiatives such as Antur Stiniog (Stiniog adventure), it has developed a number of projects with the aim of regenerating the town, including a world-class mountain bike downhill course.

The River of Slate is a pavement sculpture opposite the railway station. It includes the names of all 350 Welsh slate mines, each engraved on a block of slate of the appropriate colour. Also near the railway station is a series of slate chiselled sculptures, each 7.5 m tall and constructed of 15,000 stacked slates. The slates are laid at an angle of 30° to match the lie of the Blaenau seams.

River of Slate, Blaenau Ffestiniog

2·2 Geology of Snowdonia

Dinorwig quarry slate galleries

North Wales displays one of Europe's thickest and most complete sequences of Cambrian, Ordovician, and Silurian strata. The geology of the Trail is dominated by slate formed during these periods. Slate is metamorphosed sedimentary rock, usually mudstone, which has been changed by great pressure and temperature due to volcanic action and movement. This has caused the rock to form parallel cleavage planes along the grain, which allow it to be split into thin, strong and impervious sheets. This is why slate is used for roofing and flooring.

The slate comes from a number of geological periods. The "superquarries" of Penrhyn (Bethesda) and Dinorwig (Llanberis) rose out of the excellent qualities of the Cambrian slate, which was formed some 600 million years ago. This same slate occurs in the Waunfawr and Nantlle districts.

The other major quarrying area of Blaenau Ffestiniog still extracts Ordovician slate formed about 450 million years ago, and named after an ancient Welsh tribe. During this period, volcanoes spewed ash and lava over the area which was to become Snowdonia.

The slate comes in many colours from the light blue-grey of Penrhyn slate, through the blue-red colour of Dinorwig slate to dark blue Ffestiniog slate. Some veins provide vivid greens and reds. Slate is not the only rock that you will see in the hills along the Trail. Outcrops of rhyolite, formed during massive volcanic eruptions in Wales in the Ordovician period, appear in the stream-bed of the River Machno which descends beside the quarry footpath. These are referred to as *rhyolitic tuffs* and often contains fragments of quartz or feldspars formed when the magma or lava from the volcanic eruption cooled. Rhyolite is a light coloured rock, and because it is acidic, very few plants can grow on its outcrops.

Long after the mountain building period, some 400 million years ago, North Wales was covered by ice during the Great Ice Age and subsequent lesser ice ages which ended 10,000 years ago. The advance and retreat of the glaciers during these ice ages and the warm periods between them carved out the U-shaped valleys of North Wales.

Typical slate scenery

Two examples of such valleys are the Machno valley and the impressive Ogwen valley with a glaciated cwm (or cirque) at its head. The short diversion from the outflow of Llyn Ogwen to Llyn Idwal will give you an impressive view of a cirque, surrounded by the towering cliffs of the Glyder range, riven by the dark, deep chasm of the Devil`s Kitchen.

Darwin and Cwm Idwal

Cwm Idwal is famous for its connection with Charles Darwin, who first visited in 1831 and noticed that some boulders next to the lake contained fossilised shells. He realised that they must have come from a prehistoric sea and had been thrown to the surface by forces deep within the earth.

Camau daearegol Darwin trwy Eryri - 1831
Darwin's geological footsteps through Snowdonia - 1831

Darwin feature, Ogwen Cottage

The rocks of Cwm Idwal were formed some 400 million years ago, when much of North Wales lay underwater and volcanoes under the seabed were particularly active. Their eruptions threw out dark basaltic and pale silica-rich rhyolitic rocks. The rocks of Cwm Idwal have interbedded marine sediments that illustrate this action.

Fascinated by his discovery, Darwin returned to Cwm Idwal and deduced that the glaciers of the ice ages had formed its impressive hanging valley. If you walk up to Llyn Idwal, notice the moraine mounds dotted around the landscape – debris left by the melting glacier. Look also for the 'rôche moutonnées' – sheepback rocks, worn smooth at their upstream end, but 'plucked' (steep) at the downstream end. You may see scoring on the surface of these rocks, caused by glacier-borne stones. For more information on Cwm Idwal and Darwin's Boulders, visit *www.geolsoc.org.uk/GeositesCwmIdwal*.

Darwin's Boulders

2·3 Snowdon

At 1085 m (3560 ft) above sea level, Snowdon (Yr Wyddfa) is the highest mountain in England and Wales. It is the most popular mountain in the UK, climbed by some 600,000 people each year, many of whom have little experience of a mountain environment. As a result, it is not unusual to see people in unsuitable footwear and lacking basic safety equipment on this high and often hostile mountain. Despite the vast crowds which invade the mountain, particularly in summer and on Bank Holidays, there are remarkably few deaths, although this number (about 10 deaths per year on average) is still far too high: nearly all are avoidable. Go up in reasonable weather with adequate footwear and equipment, follow the well-defined paths and observe the Mountain Code: see page 23.

The climb is well worth the effort, with magnificent summit views of the imposing Snowdon Horseshoe and the ranges beyond. The summit café is a recent development, replacing the building designed by Clough Williams Ellis, whose distinctive turquoise corporate colour appears also in the Croesor valley and at Conwy Falls Café, Betws-y-Coed.

Several routes lead to the summit from the Trail, any of which could be completed as an out-and-back hike. However, use of the Snowdon Sherpa bus makes for a more interesting expedition. If hours of daylight are a concern, catch an early bus to allow for a flexible return hike.   For the round trip including bus ride, allow 5-8 hours, plus a margin for safety.

From Llanberis, take the Snowdon Sherpa bus to Pen y Pass car park and make a choice: bear right for the exhilarating Pyg Track to traverse steep crags below the ridge of Crib Goch. Alternatively, bear left along the Miners' Track to ascend through the enclosed cwm of the Snowdon Horseshoe, passing the lakes of Llydaw and Glaslyn.

Panorama from Snowdon

The two routes converge at about 750 m and reach the summit within about 3·4 mi/5·3 km from the car park. For an easy descent (4·7 mi/7·5 km) with a refreshment stop on the way, follow the Llanberis Path heading north-west beside the 120-year-old mountain railway.

Alternatively, for one of the easier ascents, from Rhyd Ddu take the Snowdon Sherpa bus or walk to Snowdon Ranger Youth Hostel beside Llyn Cwellyn 1·4 mi/2·2 km away. From here, follow the Snowdon Ranger Path for 4·0 mi/6·4 km. The route zig-zags uphill, with impressive views of the towering crags of Clogwyn Du'r Arddu. Descend along the south ridge of the Rhyd Ddu Path for a total of 3·7 mi/5·9 km: be sure to bear off right (west) along the Llechog ridge, rather than continuing south towards the prominent peak of Yr Aran. This ridge descent has some relatively exposed steep ground on your left, but will not faze the average walker. The route ends outside the Cwellyn Arms and nearby tea shop.

The Mountain Code

To report an accident dial 999 or 112 and ask for Police, then Mountain Rescue

Before you set off

- Learn to use map and compass.
- Learn the mountain distress signals.
- Know basic first aid and the symptoms of exposure.
- Plan within your abilities.
- Do not pollute water.
- Avoid going alone unless you have relevant experience.
- Check the weather forecast before committing yourself.

When you set off

- Leave details of your route and check in after you return to safety.
- Take windproofs, waterproofs, first aid kit and survival bag.
- Wear suitable footwear and clothing for the conditions.
- Take suitable map, compass, torch, whistle, food and drink.

2·4 The Great Little Trains of Wales

Penrhyn Quarry Railway

The original railway was built in 1798-1801 for horse-drawn wagons and included three inclines (steep cable-drawn railways to lower trucks down from the quarry). Trains of up to 24 wagons, each carrying a ton of slates, were hauled along the railway by teams of two or three horses. The construction of a standard gauge branch from Bangor to Bethesda threatened to offer minor quarries in the Ogwen valley cheaper transport for their slates, so Baron Penrhyn was forced to improve his transport route and the 1 ft 11 in gauge line was upgraded to allow steam powered trains in 1879. The line closed in 1962.

Locomotive Charles at Penrhyn Castle

Dinorwig and Padarn Railways

While the Penrhyn quarry tramway began operation in 1801, slate from Dinorwig was being hauled down by sledge to Llyn Padarn and transferred to horse-drawn carts at the end of the lake. In 1809 Thomas Assheton-Smith took control of the quarry, with the business expanding rapidly. However, it was 1821 before a horse-drawn tramway was constructed to carry slates to Port Dinorwig on the Menai Strait. With a difference of 1000 feet between the quarry and the port, nearly twice that at Penrhyn quarry, the tramway required significant inclines.

This route started high up in the quarry, but became redundant when Assheton-Smith built the Padarn Railway. This four-foot gauge line was initially horse-drawn with wagons being lowered the last 300 feet to the dockside down an incline. Steam locomotives were introduced in 1848. Passengers were never carried, but quarrymen travelled the line using human-powered vehicles. An example of one of these can be seen at the National Slate Museum. The line closed in 1961.

Ten years later, a short length re-opened alongside the lake for visitors, extending into Llanberis in 2003. Once again, the three original Dinorwig quarry locomotives – Dolbadarn, Elidir and Thomas Bach – steam through the preserved quarry workings of Gilfach Ddu and the visitor can enjoy a five-mile trip beside the lake.

Snowdon Mountain Railway

When plans were put forward for a railway to the top of Snowdon from Rhyd Ddu, there were fears that Llanberis would lose its tourist trade. Local landowner George William Duff Assheton-Smith, who owned Dinorwig quarry, allowed his land to be used for a competing proposal: on 16 November 1894 the Snowdon Mountain Tramroad and Hotels Co Ltd was formed.

Snowdon Mountain Railway

The railway used a rack and pinion system patented by a German engineer, Dr Roman Abt. Five steam engines were bought from Switzerland and four of these original locomotives are still at work: Enid, Wyddfa (Welsh for Snowdon), Snowdon and Moel Siabod.

Welsh Highland Railway

Owners of slate workings near Beddgelert had high hopes, even though their businesses were dwarfed by mighty Penrhyn and Dinorwig. Many companies built short sections of railway, or aspired to do so, but it was the Portmadoc, Beddgelert and South Snowdon Railway that gained most momentum. In 1903, this company purchased the North Wales Power & Electric Traction Company with the aim of using electric traction on their steep inclines.

Welsh Highland Railway

By 1906 much of the trackbed and tunnels had been prepared with hopes of linking Porthmadog with Caernarfon. This project became the Welsh Highland Railway, which opened fully in 1923, using 50-year old rolling stock serving a sparse population and a dwindling slate industry. The railway limped from crisis to crisis, eventually going into receivership in 1933 and liquidation in 1941.

In the meantime, the line lay in the hands of the receiver and the trackbed was never undesignated as a railway. In 1998, the Ffestiniog Railway Company (FRC) commenced restoration. The completed line now extends from Caernarfon to FRC's Porthmadog station making it possible to travel all the way from Caernarfon to Blaenau Ffestiniog by narrow-gauge railway. The restoration project was a massive endeavour involving professionals and volunteers, with rail purchased from India and huge Beyer-Garrett steam engines from South Africa.

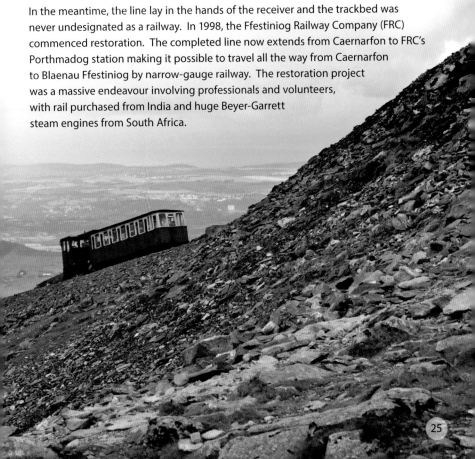

Ffestiniog Railway

This railway opened in 1835 as a horse-drawn tramway. The wagons were taken up and over the hill west of Tanygrisiau lake on two inclines. These were superseded by the Moelwyn tunnel which bore straight through the hill in 1842. This gave the railway a downward gradient all the way from Blaenau Ffestiniog to the Cob, a narrow causeway across the Glaslyn estuary in Porthmadog. Trains of up to 100 wagons rolled down the line under gravity, carrying horses to take the train over the Cob and to haul the empty wagons back up to Blaenau Ffestiniog.

The Ffestiniog Railway allowed the remote village of Blaenau Ffestiniog to become a major international supplier of slate and let Porthmadog develop as an important regional port. With the construction of a standard-gauge line to Porthmadog from the south, the Ffestiniog Railway saw the potential and adapted the line for steam passenger services. By 1865, the slogan was 'Breakfast in Blaenau – Tea in London'. 1863 saw the introduction of the unusual Double Fairlie locomotives, of which Myrddin Emrys (built in 1879 in Boston Lodge, Porthmadog) is a fine example.

The line closed in 1946 but was reopened over the following 10 years and in 1958 it reached Tan y Bwlch. In the mid-1950s, Tanygrisiau reservoir was extended as part of a pumped storage hydro-electricity scheme, flooding the railway and its tunnel. Not to be thwarted, in the early 1970s volunteers constructed a spiral section of track near Dduallt to gain height, and built a diversion above the lake to rejoin the original line at Tanygrisiau near the Lakeside Café.

Ffestiniog Railway

2·5 Habitats and wildlife

The Snowdonia Slate Trail passes
through three main habitat types:

- river valley and pasture
- woodland and forest
- moorland and mountain

Brown hare

River valley and pasture

The mudflats of Penrhyn Bay, on the Menai Strait, are
home to seabirds including oystercatchers, dunlin, terns, and
many types of gull. Curlews spend their winter on the estuary before turning to the
high moorlands In summer. Their burbling call is probably one of the most evocative
of birdsongs, and their long curved beaks the most impressive.

Dipper

On the inland rivers, you may glimpse the
blue flash of a kingfisher, or the darting
dipper as it fearlessly hunts small fish in
fast-flowing waters. Grey herons hunt either
standing stock still on the edge of the water,
or sometimes gliding low above the surface.

In the open fields, you are less likely to
spot animals, hidden as they are in the
undergrowth and below ground. Field
margins provide habitat for brown hares and small mammals such as field voles,
which support barn owls and kestrels. They also offer nesting and feeding sites for
birds such as corn buntings and skylarks.

Common flowers in field margins are an important source of pollen and nectar for
bees and other insects. These margins are also home to insects and small mammals,
feeding areas for owls and other birds of prey, in particular buzzards. Unfortunately,
local agriculture tends to depend on cattle and, more often, sheep, which tend to
impoverish the diversity of field margin habitats.

The sheep that you'll see are mainly hardy Welsh Mountain sheep, with thick, white
fleeces and long tails. After spring lambing, they spend their summers in the hills and
mountains before descending in late autumn to be fattened up. Increasingly, they are
being crossbred with Texel – a sturdy sheep with a short snub-nosed face, white close
fleece and black hooves. The hybrid provides meat of high quality.

Welsh mountain sheep

Woodland and forest

Gwydir is a mixed forest which combines some of Wales's finest oak glades together with large areas of conifers (Douglas fir and Norway spruce). As you walk through the woods, look above you for signs of buzzards, peregrines, merlins and goshawks. Other birds in the area include meadow pipits, wheatears and ring ouzels. You are unlikely to see the very rare black grouse. However, in the Machno valley you may well sight a red kite – a large bird of prey distinguished by its forked tail.

Red kite

The Trail passes through gorges surrounded by mixed woodland of oak, alder and elm, where bullfinches, lesser spotted woodpeckers, marsh tits, song thrushes, spotted flycatchers, tree pipits and willow tits may be seen. Unfortunately, these populations have declined greatly over the past decades as have those of dunnocks, goldcrests, lesser redpolls, mistle thrushes, willow warblers and wood warblers.

You may be lucky enough to spot a red squirrel in the trees of the Ogwen valley. Populations of this native species have been re-introduced where the high ground helps to shield reds from the threat of grey squirrels. The grey squirrel is its larger, non-native cousin and it outcompetes them for food, and also carries squirrelpox – a disease that is deadly to reds but harmless to greys.

Red squirrel

The pine marten is present in the wooded foothills of Snowdon, although they are seldom seen. Sightings have been reported around Waunfawr. The pine marten is the only animal agile enough to prey on squirrels, and happily they take grey squirrels rather than the smaller, lighter reds.

Pine marten

Moorland and mountain

Snowdonia has fine moorland wildernesses, particularly between Waunfawr and Nantlle and between Cwm Cynfal and Cwm Penmachno. These areas are home to a variety of wildlife including mountain goats, ravens and choughs, as well as the occasional polecat and stoat.

No one knows how the Welsh mountain goat came to live on the mountains of Snowdonia, but you may see them in Parc Padarn, above Llanberis, around Beddgelert or clinging to the rocks on Tryfan. These hardy beasts have swept back horns, black and white shaggy coats and beards, and they thrive in the harshest conditions. They eat almost any vegetation, helping them to survive the winters.

Wild mountain goat

Chough

Snowdonia is a haven for various members of the crow family, including the jet-black raven with its powerful black bill and distinctive 'pruk! pruk!' call. You may be lucky enough to glimpse the elusive chough, a smaller member of the crow family. It has a more delicate bill, and its bill and legs are red unlike any other crow. Its name evokes its distinctive 'chee-uff' call and it performs acrobatic aerial displays. Numbers in the UK were in sharp decline, but have started to recover – particularly in Wales where low-intensity livestock farming takes place near suitable nesting sites. When walking through heather moorland, you may startle a well-camouflaged red grouse, which will take off suddenly with its 'ge-back' call. Grouse feed on young heather shoots and nest in more mature heather. There is little, if any, shooting on these moors, so they are not managed, but generally are grazed by the ubiquitous sheep.

Red grouse

Another rare creature, difficult to spot, is Britain's most beautiful beetle, the Snowdon or rainbow leaf beetle, named after its stripes of red, yellow, blue and green. It relies on wild thyme for its survival, and is highly endangered with an adult population of only about 1000.

The Snowdon lily is Britain's rarest plant, found in only five locations, all high in Snowdonia. It is only about 5 inches (12 cm) tall with small white flowers and thin spidery leaves. Its other names are spiderwort or, in Welsh, 'brwynddail y mynydd' or 'rush-leaved mountain plant'.

Snowdon beetle

It is known to botanists as Lloydia serotina, after Edward Llwyd, the pioneer of Welsh botany who discovered it in about 1688. An ice age relic, it is threatened by climate change and there may be fewer than 100 bulbs left. There are plans to introduce the plant to suitable sites in Scotland before it becomes extinct. In Snowdonia it flowers from late May to early July and grows in sheltered ledges and rock faces well away from grazing animals.

Snowdon lily, © SNPA

Snowdonia is also home to many Arctic plants, including alpine meadow grass, tufted saxifrage, alpine saxifrage, purple saxifrage, alpine woodsia and alpine cinquefoil. These may be seen on the sections between Croesor and Tanygrisiau and between Cwm Cynfal and Cwm Penmachno, as well as on the moorland above Capel Curig.

Purple saxifrage

3·1 Bangor to Bethesda

Distance	6·3 miles 10·2 km
Terrain	a mixture of paved cycle path, country lanes, woodland tracks, and field paths
Grade	some modest ascents and descents
Food & drink	Bethesda
Side trip	Penrhyn Castle
Summary	starting from the sea at Port Penrhyn, this introduction to Snowdonia scenery takes you to the slate village of Bethesda, with extensive views of the Carnedd and Glyder mountain ranges en route

	2·1	Llandegai	2·8	Llanllechid	1·5	
Bangor	3·3		4·5		2·4	Bethesda

The Trail starts on the outskirts of Bangor, from Port Penrhyn, which is 2·4 km from the railway station and 1·6 km from the bus station.

- Walk along Bangor's High Street to its eastern end, then turn right to follow the main road for about 150 m. Turn left at the end of the public gardens into the port area. There are plans to create a monument here, but as of early 2018 the start is unmarked.

- The Trail begins along Lôn Las Ogwen (Ogwen green lane), a tree-lined cycleway. Follow this for 2·2 km to pass under a small road bridge. Immediately turn right to cross this bridge.

Penrhyn Castle: see page 32

Lôn Las Ogwen

- Continue along the lane for about 800 m and turn right through a kissing-gate. At the main road, take the 'North Wales Path' (not the 'Wales Coast Path'), and turn into a gravel drive, past houses on your right. The mountains beckon ahead.

- Go through the gate at the end of the drive, following the hedge until you reach the fence alongside the A55. Keep this to your right, and continue straight along a concrete track under the A55.

- Descend the path to the left after the crash barrier and cross the Afon Ogwen, where you may be lucky enough to spot a kingfisher among the pools.

- Look out for the millwheel. Walk up Cochwillan Mill drive and turn right up a stony path into the fields. The grassy path hugs the field boundary on your left before passing through a gap in the wall. Behind you, Penrhyn Castle, a Victorian folly, towers above the trees: see panel. ❶

Penrhyn Castle
Penrhyn Castle was built between 1821 and 1837 by the architect Thomas Hopper for George Hay-Dawkins Pennant. This Norman-style building became the home of Lord Penrhyn, owner of Penrhyn quarry. Now owned by the National Trust, it is worth a visit to appreciate the quarry owner's wealth created by the labour of local quarrymen. The extensive and beautiful gardens were designed by Walter Speed of Great Abington, Cambridgeshire, who became head gardener at the castle in 1862 and remained there for 58 years. For visit details, see www.nationaltrust.org.uk.

- On reaching the farm track, leave the North Wales Path and turn right through the gate. Walk along the drive until it veers off right, and continue along the field boundary to a field gate. Cross the field diagonally, aiming for the trees over to the right.

- A clear path runs alongside the wood, reaching the A5 at Halfway Bridge, ❷ about halfway between Bethesda and Bangor (mile 3·7). Note the slate fences, which are typical of this area.

- Cross the busy road with care, and go left for about 150 m along the footpath. Cross the road again and take the footpath opposite, marked Pandy Isaf (lower textile mill).

- The wide track passes two cottages on the right. Bear left along the gravel track and left again along the path through the woods until you reach a farm track.

Halfway Bridge

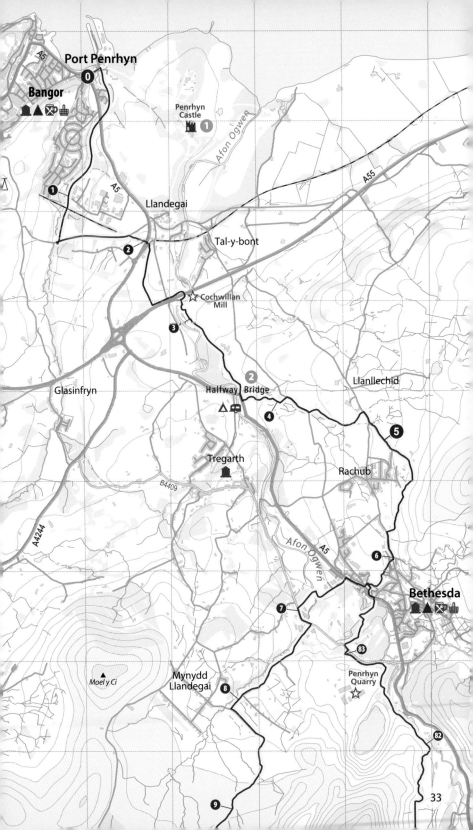

Port Penrhyn

Bangor

Penrhyn
Castle 1

0

A6

A5

1

Afon Ogwen

Llandegai

A55

2

Tal-y-bont

☆ Cochwillan
Mill

3

2

Halfway Bridge

4

Llanllechid

5

Glasinfryn

Tregarth

Rachub

B4409

Afon Ogwen

A5

6

A4244

Bethesda

7

83

Moel y Ci

Mynydd
Llandegai

8

Penrhyn
Quarry
☆

82

9

33

Avenue leading to Llanllechid church

- Turn left here, and reach a lane, where you turn right to follow it for 300 m. Here, a footpath crosses the fields to the left, eventually reaching Llanllechid church. Divert through the churchyard to see the mountains above Bethesda and the tumbling, blue slate tips of Penrhyn Quarry.

- To return to the Trail, follow the church's yew-lined drive with intricately carved slate gravestones to the road. Turn right to the junction in the village centre. Bear left along the lane between the houses, and bear left again at Cae'r Groes road, to pass the Tan y Bwlch outdoor safety training centre.

- A grass track then leads you onto the hillside with panoramic views over Bethesda, the Carnedd and Glyder ranges, and the extensive Penrhyn quarry, which is still operational and a major feature of the landscape.

- Go through the gate, turn right and, at the level area of the old quarry workings, bear left to reach a gate to the right of a fenced underground reservoir. A clear path descends the hill.

- Where the path becomes indistinct in a field of boulders, aim for the gate to the left of the farm buildings: walk down to the road and turn left.

- Immediately before the pub Y Sior, descend steps to the street. Go through a gate into the field and take the path to the left, emerging into a car park. Walk along the car park entrance and turn left to reach Bethesda High Street with its friendly Caffi Coed y Brenin (king's wood café), a social enterprise.

The boulder field

3·2 Bethesda to Llanberis

Distance	7·2 miles 11·6 km
Terrain	country lanes, open high moorland tracks and paths (boggy in parts), woodland and field paths and broad farm tracks
Grade	moderate ascent from Bethesda to Mynydd Llandegai followed by open moorland and an easy descent to Llanberis
Food & drink	Lodge Dinorwig, Llanberis
Side trip	National Slate Museum, Llanberis
Summary	an interesting walk through the slate landscape around Bethesda and Llanberis over the wild Gwaun Gynfi moors, with the option to visit the excellent National Slate Museum of Wales

Bethesda	1·7	Mynydd Llandegai	3·5		Dinorwig	2·0	Llanberis
	2·8		5·6			3·2	

- At the High Street, turn right towards the north end of Bethesda, and reach a grocery store. Turn left into Station Road, and go straight ahead to pick up a footpath alongside the river.

- At the bridge, cross the river and go straight up through the trees. Turn left when you reach the main road.

- Walk along the road for about 250 m beneath the towering slate walls of the historic Felin Fawr (large mill). Here the main slate workshops of the Penrhyn quarry were located alongside the Penrhyn Quarry Railway terminus.

- At the Bradite paint works, turn right in the direction of Mynydd Llandegai. Continue along this road for about 1·5 km, passing the reservoir which supplied the two waterwheels (which still exist) at Felin Fawr.

Bridge over Afon Ogwen

- Continue uphill until you reach a T-junction. Behind is a panoramic view of the hills and mountains encircling Bethesda

- Go left along Gefnan road to a gate at its end. Continue onwards along the track which bends to the right, leading to a kissing-gate at the wall junction.

- Follow a slightly sunken track that veers left and crosses open moorland, with views ahead of the main Snowdon mountain range.

- After keeping to this track for nearly 1 km, cross a stream near the retaining embankment of a reservoir, Llyn Owen-y-ddol. The track meets another stream and keeps to its right bank, becoming narrower and heading towards a pumping station visible on the horizon.

- Continue alongside the stream until you reach an unusual feature where two streams appear to cross. Go straight over to what appears to be the minor incoming stream.

- From here, the Trail becomes more indistinct. Continue straight ahead, following waymarkers. Where this stream divides, cross its right fork and aim for a wall slightly over to the right.

Crossing Gwaun Gynfi moor

- After crossing two more streams, aim for an ancient slate and iron stile on the near horizon, just left of a telegraph pole ahead.

- Cross the stile and look for a slate post in the middle of the featureless moorland. Keep the wall, then a fence, on your right, and (trying to avoid wet areas) go around a number of small ponds on your left, just before a farm track. Make for the road ahead.

- Turn right along the road, but where it veers right, leave it to make a left-right dogleg down a lane. At the access to Tan-y-Buarth farm, take the path on the left. Cross the fields and walk along the clear grassy path.

The Trail above Deiniolen

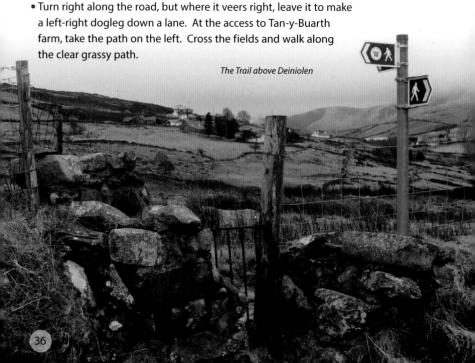

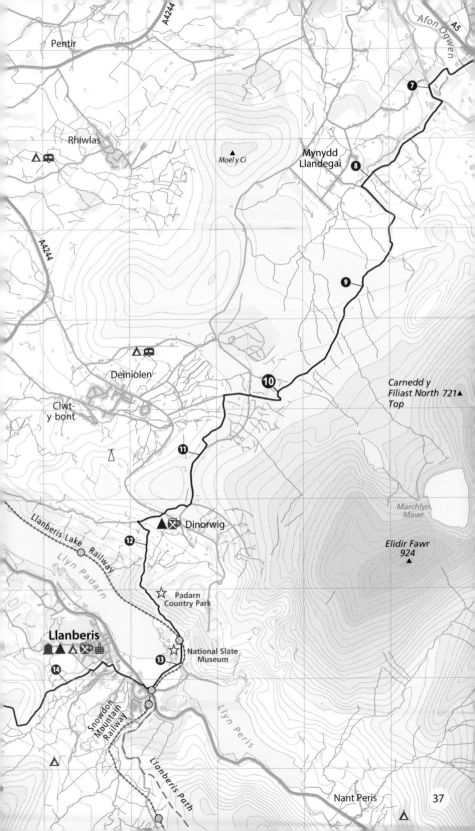

Pentir

Rhiwlas

A4244

A4244

Moel y Ci

Mynydd
Llandegai

7

8

9

Deiniolen

Clwt-
y-bont

Carnedd y
Filiast North 721▲
Top

10

11

Marchlyn
Mawr

Dinorwig

Elidir Fawr
924
▲

12

Llanberis Lake Railway

Llyn Padarn

Padarn
Country Park

☆

Llanberis

☆ National Slate
Museum

13

14

Snowdon
Mountain
Railway

Llyn Peris

Llanberis Path

Nant Peris

37

- Pass in front of a white house, then descend to a wooden gate on the right. Go through it, following the wall to a metal gate. Turn left up the concrete drive.

- Turn right to meet the road and turn right again for about 700 m to a track in front of Sardis Chapel.

- Follow the track for 120 m, then turn left on a path just before the house. This becomes an attractive, narrow path between a wall and

Lodge Dinorwig café and bunkhouse

slate fence, with impressive views of Llyn Padarn and Snowdon beyond.

- Reach the road at the former school, now Lodge Dinorwig, with refreshment and accommodation available. The Trail continues steeply downhill on the lane opposite.

- At a signpost on your right to Deiniolen, turn into the lane to the left and soon reach a half sunken cottage on your right.

- Immediately after it, a footpath on the right joins a steep downhill track. At its sharp right hairpin bend, leave it to go ahead into the woods. Cross a metal footbridge and enter Padarn Country Park.

- Within the woodland, where you may be lucky enough to see feral goats, keep to the yellow waymarked route until you reach a fork. Bear right, at first along the blue and yellow route, then following the yellow and green waymarkers.

- At the next fork, bear right along the green route to a junction. Here, a wide track on the right zigzags past the quarry hospital, now part of the National Slate Museum. The tarmac drive takes you to a building: descend the rough path to its right.

- Cross the base of an impressive restored steep incline (a cable-operated railway to lower trucks from the quarry above) and make for the Llanberis Lake Railway station.

National Slate Museum

- From the museum complex, follow the road to the left. Before the railway crosses the road, turn right along a footpath leading to Llanberis, going parallel to the Llanberis Lake Railway.
- Turn right at the main road and then left towards the village centre. The Trail then turns left into Tŷ Du Road. To visit the village centre for accommodation and supplies, instead continue along the main road (High Street).

National Slate Museum
Housed in the former slate workshops of the vast Dinorwig quarry, the museum complex also features Wales' largest working water wheel. Before entering its car park, go through the short tunnel to your left to experience the towering cliffs of the Vivian quarry with its deep blue pool and overhead cableway. The workshop exhibits bring to life the story of the slate industry and its people. Admission is free and there are also talks and slate-splitting demonstrations. For visit details, see **www.museum.wales/slate**.

Llyn Padarn and the Snowdon range

39

3·3 Llanberis to Beddgelert

Distance	**20·0 miles 32·2 km**
Terrain	country lanes, exposed moorland tracks, woodland paths, broad farm tracks and a modern constructed path section
Grade	a tough section, including a steep ascent out of the Nantlle valley, then easy paths through the Gwyrfai valley
Food & drink	Waunfawr (check opening hours), Rhyd Ddu, Beddgelert
Side trip	Welsh Highland Railway,
Summary	an exhilarating day involving steep ascents to high moorland and descents into broad valleys, with impressive views of the coast and mountains, ending with level walking to Beddgelert

```
        3·8  Waunfawr        5·9       Nantlle    5·1   Rhyd Ddu   5·2
Llanberis 6·1              9·5                   8·2              8·4   Beddgelert
```

- From the village centre, return to Tŷ Du Road, then turn left into Fron Goch road. At the top, turn right then left to ascend a narrow lane with widening views of the Dinorwig quarry and Glyder range behind, and with the Snowdon massif to the left.

- After about 1 km, the lane becomes a track that continues to the right, contouring the hillside at high level. Views open up of the Llanberis lakes, the coastal plain and Anglesey beyond.

Dinorwig quarry and the Snowdon range

- Keep to this track and continue between the forestry and high slate tips. About 750 m along the lane past the woods, take the drive on your left through a galvanised gate signed 'North Wales Pilgrim's Way'. The Pilgrim's Way, which runs from Holywell to Bardsey Island, is waymarked and shares the route of our Trail for some distance.

- After passing the second white cottage on this drive, go through a gate and turn right down a track running alongside a deep dry streambed. After bending to the left, the track bears to the right above a small cottage with a black tarred roof.

- When this track veers to the left, leave it to the right at the signed public footpath through the fields. After crossing a stream, continue through fields, temporarily joining a tarmac drive downhill for about 50 m.

- As the drive bears off to the left, leave it to go straight ahead along the waymarked route. The path then passes between a wall and a small stream, and through a kissing-gate near a ruin.

- After going through further gates, pass to the left of a white house along a path between low walls. If you want to detour to Antur Waunfawr and its café (mile 17·5), go about 100 m up to your right. Otherwise cross the lane and follow the narrow path until you reach a street.

- Turn right here and, after about 80 m, turn left down a footpath opposite house number 24, bringing you to the main road (A4085).

Caffi Blas y Waun, Antur Waunfawr

- Follow the A4085 to the left, crossing the Afon Gwyrfai and the Welsh Highland Railway, one of the Great Little Trains of Wales, to reach Snowdonia Park Inn, which has its own micro-brewery.

- After passing the pub's car park, take the lane right signposted to Rhosgadfan. After about 400 m, take the footpath on the left, signposted 'Y Fron 3¼ mls'. This track can be somewhat overgrown with bracken.

Wooden ladder-stile above Waunfawr

- Climb steadily uphill, keeping to the left to enter the woods opposite a very large boulder. Go over two wooden ladder-stiles over stone walls.

- The path then crosses a further stile and goes over a boulder field, then through gaps in walls around a series of small enclosures.

- This ancient track passes the remains of a settlement on the left and goes into another enclosure. Continue upwards to a gate as the enclosure narrows between stone walls, and take the stony path opposite.

- The path goes through heather towards a walled area. Aim for the left corner of this area, following the clear track alongside.

- The track becomes indistinct as it nears a large white house on the right: follow the house's driveway and turn left. The surfaced track passes Hafod Ruffydd farm and becomes unsurfaced, next to an unusual rock garden. Continue ahead along the track.

- As the track veers right, bear left on a grassy trail: a sign on a slate slab on the ground announces 'Betws Garmon'. Reach a footpath crossing marked Moel Smytho and Pen y Gaer to the left. Go right along the clear path through the heather.

- Follow this path as it tends to the left for a short distance along an obvious long hollow (probably a trial quarry excavation) before resuming the original direction. As you come over a slight rise you will see a huge boulder. To the left is the looming mass of Mynydd Mawr.

- Go right, around the boulder, continuing with the slate tips to your right. Look ahead for waymarkers; the Nantlle Ridge forms a dramatic skyline to the left.

- The path circles the base of a slate tip before ascending to the right onto it. Take to the main quarry road which turns left soon after leaving the workings.

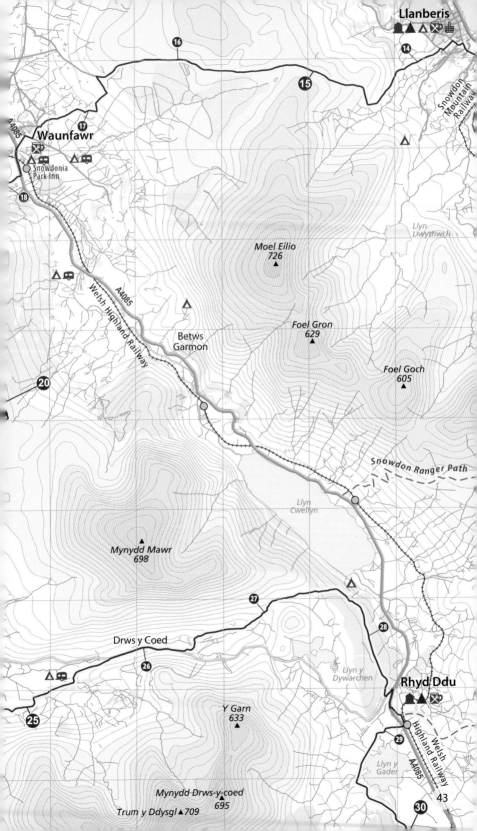

Llanberis

Waunfawr

Snowdonia
Park Inn

Snowdon
Mountain
Railway

Welsh Highland Railway

A4085

Moel Eilio
726 ▲

Foel Gron
629 ▲

Foel Goch
605 ▲

Llyn
Dwythwch

Betws
Garmon

Snowdon Ranger Path

Llyn
Cwellyn

Mynydd Mawr
698 ▲

Drws y Coed

Llyn y
Dywarchen

Rhyd Ddu

Y Garn
633 ▲

Welsh Highland Railway

A4085

Llyn y
Gader

Mynydd Drws-y-coed
695 ▲

Trum y Ddysgl ▲ 709

43

- Cross the cattle grid and bear right towards a cottage, passing to its left, and to the right of the next building. Continue down a narrow field towards a large flooded quarry pit. Pass this on its left along a slate-fenced path.

- Follow a narrow grassy path alongside, and to the right of, the wall. After crossing a drive on your left, you will reach a kissing-gate on the left. Pass through this and walk down alongside the row of cottages ahead to the road.

- The Trail now goes right, then left, down the footpath alongside the former school until you reach another road. This school building is now a community hub, incorporating a small shop, café and well-positioned bunkhouse.

Dorothea quarry

- Cross the road to the right and pass through a kissing-gate, crossing the field to a further gate – in spring, this field hosts a mass of wild flowers. Climb a flight of slate steps onto a raised track or tramway and follow this to the left until you reach the chain link fence.

- Ignore the stile, and instead find the faint path to the left of the fence. This leads through two kissing-gates below a high slate wall to your right.

- Cross the field diagonally to its far right corner and go through another kissing-gate. Walk down the field and alongside the fence down a narrow section separating two impressive quarry pits.

Nantlle ridge from Pen yr Orsedd quarry

- Pass through a gap in the wall near a stile, go down some steps, and make for a gate to your right. You are now in the heart of the Nantlle slate quarries, which have operated since the 1300s.

- Follow a narrow path at the base of the slate tip to your right, climbing slightly to a level grassy area with the quarry over to the right. Pass the remains of buildings and the next tip on the right to reach another level grassy area.

Quarry remains above Nantlle

- After some further remains on your right, down to your left you will see the skeleton of a large building, a slate mill, where slate was cut and split.

- Opposite the far end wall, look out for a hidden, narrow path doubling back on itself to the left. This passes down a gorse-covered ramp to the level of the building.

- Walk along the grassy path alongside the slate mill to a gate between two slate tips and then descend the clear path ahead.

- Passing a tall chimney and a derelict house on your right, join a track and descend left past many abandoned buildings. Keep left at the next junction then, at the next track, turn left between two high slate walls.

- Continue, always keeping to the left, passing through a new metal gate. When you reach a lane, pass a row of cottages on the left to reach the B4418 (mile 23·4).

- Turn right along the B4418 for about 450 m to reach the drive to Ffridd farm on the left. Before you reach the farm, there is an imposing view up the Nantlle valley, with Mynydd Mawr to the left and the lofty Nantlle ridge to the right.

- Follow the drive, which becomes a grass path leading to a gate and then a good track along the valley floor. Take the stone farm track until you reach the end of Llyn Nantlle Uchaf.

- At the end of the lake, leave the track and continue straight ahead across the fields, passing through a farm gate and aiming for the stile over the wall ahead. Cross the stile and follow the track with the fence to your right.

- The track leaves the field and leads to Tal y Mignedd Isaf farm and campsite. Carry on to the right of the farmyard. After passing the campsite, take the left fork over the river and follow the drive back to the B4418.

- Turn right, passing through the small settlement of Drws-y-Coed, and then left down Drws y Coed Isaf farm drive next to a large solitary fir tree about 400 m further on.

- Walk along the concrete drive and cross a stile at a footpath sign just next to the farmyard. Footpath signs and waymarkers indicate the way across a boulder slope to a further stile.

- The grassy track passes an unusual stone structure in the field down to your right. The track itself soon veers steeply left, but your path continues ahead alongside the wall to a stile. It carries on, faint in places, on the upper side of the rushes, to a waymark post near a hawthorn bush on the near horizon.

- For a while you will have the comfort of the stream and waymarkers to guide you. Follow the waymarkers above the boggy area just below the dam wall, and pass around the drained reservoir to another stile

- Cross the field diagonally uphill to the left to the stile on the skyline. Looking back, you will see Llyn y Dywarchen ❶ and the Nantlle valley.

- Cross into the woods and follow the path down the firebreak, turning right onto a good level path. This path contours the hillside and boasts wonderful views of Snowdon to the left.

- The path widens, becoming a track and then a forest road until it meets the B4418 again. Turn down to the left for Rhyd Ddu (mile 28·7), where you can buy refreshments at the Cwellyn Arms or the Tŷ Mawr tea room.

Llyn y Dywarchen from the South ❶

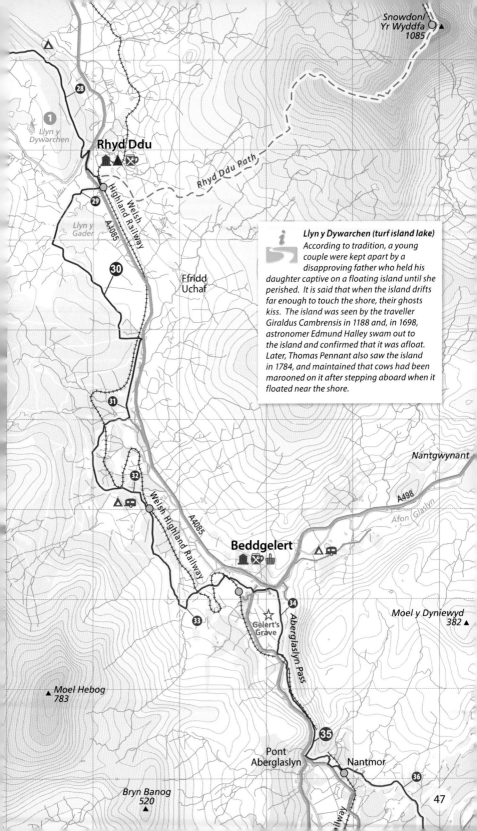

Snowdon/
Yr Wyddfa
1085

28

1

Llyn y
Dywarchen

Rhyd Ddu

Rhyd Ddu Path

29

Welsh Highland Railway

A4085

Llyn y
Gader

30

Ffridd
Uchaf

> ### Llyn y Dywarchen (turf island lake)
> According to tradition, a young couple were kept apart by a disapproving father who held his daughter captive on a floating island until she perished. It is said that when the island drifts far enough to touch the shore, their ghosts kiss. The island was seen by the traveller Giraldus Cambrensis in 1188 and, in 1698, astronomer Edmund Halley swam out to the island and confirmed that it was afloat. Later, Thomas Pennant also saw the island in 1784, and maintained that cows had been marooned on it after stepping aboard when it floated near the shore.

31

Nantgwynant

32

A498

Afon Glaslyn

Welsh Highland Railway

A4085

Beddgelert

34

Moel y Dyniewyd
382 ▲

33

Gelert's
Grave

Aberglaslyn Pass

▲ Moel Hebog
783

35

Pont
Aberglaslyn

Nantmor

36

Bryn Banog
520
▲

- Walk past the tea room and, 80 m further on, turn left to the rear of some houses to reach the railway station, toilets and car park. Opposite the car park, take the well-engineered Lôn Gwyrfai path which is waymarked all the way to Beddgelert..

- When the main path comes in from the right, turn left along this multi-user trail (walking, cycling and horse-riding). Continue on a narrow causeway around Llyn y Gader.

- Cross the Welsh Highland Railway and go right along a broad track just before the main road. Pass a car park on your right, and head towards a small wooden chalet.

- After passing a house, Hafod Ruffydd Isaf, the Trail is signed Beddgelert. Cross Pont Rhyd, the 1778 packhorse bridge, and continue straight ahead.

- Cross the railway again and pass Hafod Ruffydd Ganol farm on the left. Take the left track at the next junction and pass the sign to Hafod Ruffydd Uchaf art gallery up on the right.

- Bear left again at the next track junction, and leave the forest track a bit further on, to cross the river. Follow a path through the woods with the river on your left, keeping left at the next junction.

- Just before the railway, pass Meillionen Campsite Halt (mile 32·2) on your left. Go right at the next junction. Leave the track to cross the stream on a wooden bridge to your left and walk along the gravel path across the hillside.

- At the T-junction of paths, near the cottage Cwm Gloch Canol, the Trail goes left along the lane, crossing the railway twice – first at the Bron Hebog crossing and again at Cwm Cloch crossing. You next reach the railway as it crosses the lane on a bridge. Just before this bridge, turn right to pass beneath the line.

- Where the path forks, take the left branch into the car park. Cross the car park into the main street of Beddgelert. Walk left through the village, passing the tourist information office, until you get to the river bridge.

Beddgelert

3·4 Beddgelert to Llan Ffestiniog

Distance	14·4 miles 23·2 km
Terrain	gorge and riverside paths, country lanes, remote and exposed moorland, mountain tracks and field paths
Grade	a tough day with a long, but easy ascents, and an undulating section from Blaenau Ffestiniog to Llan Ffestiniog
Food & drink	Croesor (check opening hours), Tanygrisiau, Blaenau Ffestiniog, Llan Ffestiniog
Side trip	Rhosydd mine remains, Cwmorthin, Blaenau Ffestiniog
Summary	a varied day starting with the Aberglaslyn Pass, leading through Croesor to remote quarries with abandoned villages beneath towering cascades of blue slate, ending with an undulating walk through the Bowydd and Teigl valleys

	4·4	Croesor	4·6	Tanygrisiau	5·4	
Beddgelert	7·2		7·4		8·6	**Llan Ffestiniog**

- Leave the main street before the bridge, passing the public toilets. Just before the Afon Glaslyn, take the path to your right signposted to Gelert's Grave. Continue beside the river, then cross it next to the railway bridge.

- Cross the railway and follow the left bank of the river through the narrow Aberglaslyn gorge along a path which crosses boulders and runs along man-made ledges and across wooden bridges.

- Note that when the river is in spate, this path could be flooded and dangerous. In that case, instead use the road from the railway bridge to rejoin the Trail at Aberglaslyn bridge.

> **Gelert's Grave**
> According to legend, this marks the final resting place of Prince Llewelyn the Great's faithful dog Gelert. Llewelyn went out hunting without Gelert, leaving his infant son in his cradle. On returning, he found the dog covered in blood and the blood-stained cradle empty. Thinking that Gelert had killed his son, Llewelyn, killed the dog only to hear his son's cry from behind the cradle, lying next to a wolf that Gelert had slain. Full of remorse, Llewelyn buried his faithful hound at this spot. Another version is that this tall story was concocted by the landlord of the Goat Hotel in the 18th century to encourage tourism.

Aberglaslyn Pass

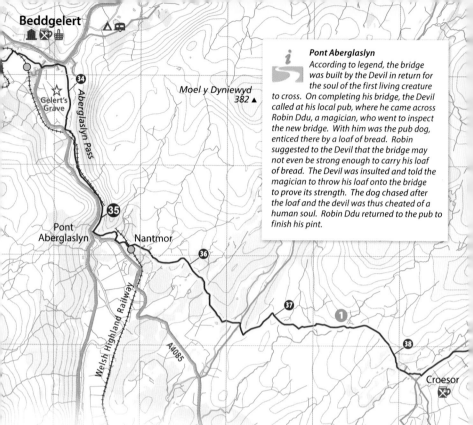

Beddgelert

Gelert's Grave

Aberglaslyn Pass

Moel y Dyniewyd
382 ▲

34

35

Pont
Aberglaslyn   Nantmor

36

37

1

38

Croesor

Welsh Highland Railway

A4085

> **Pont Aberglaslyn**
> According to legend, the bridge was built by the Devil in return for the soul of the first living creature to cross. On completing his bridge, the Devil called at his local pub, where he came across Robin Ddu, a magician, who went to inspect the new bridge. With him was the pub dog, enticed there by a loaf of bread. Robin suggested to the Devil that the bridge may not even be strong enough to carry his loaf of bread. The Devil was insulted and told the magician to throw his loaf onto the bridge to prove its strength. The dog chased after the loaf and the devil was thus cheated of a human soul. Robin Ddu returned to the pub to finish his pint.

- Just before the riverside path meets the road at Pont Aberglaslyn, ascend left up steps: the path ahead lies high above the road. When you see a cottage down on the right, take the left fork uphill, before descending to a car park near the railway.

- When you leave the car park, turn left onto the road (A4085). Almost immediately turn left again into a narrow lane signed Nantmor, which zigzags steeply uphill, crossing the Welsh Highland Railway at a level crossing.

- Pass Peniel chapel on the left, keeping along the lane for about 2 km to reach a T-junction. Here, cross the road to a stony track bounded by stone walls.

- Go through the gate and follow this track, a former drove road used for taking animals to market. The route is well-defined at all times, but can be wet in places and leads onto the open hillside.

- Eventually, this track joins another well used path, signposted to Cnicht on the left. The way is straight ahead, eventually reaching the tarmac lane into Croesor village.

Drovers' road to Croesor

Croesor valley

- Cross the footbridge over the river on the right into the car park with toilet. Go through the car park to the Croesor café and art gallery.

- Turn left up the lane, taking the right fork up the stony track near a row of houses, Bryn Hyfryd. This climbs a wide quarry track steadily upwards, coming to a stile into the workings of Croesor mine.

- Pass a number of ruined buildings on the right: one features a semi-circular cast iron beam, probably part of a mill wheel assembly. Keeping the tip and the remains of the integrated mill on your left, you reach more ruins on the right. The broad track becomes a narrow path, turning right through these ruins, and wending its way up the hillside, above the mine workings.

- The path, paved or stepped in places, tends to the left, always climbing the steep craggy hillside to reach the highest point on the Trail. The path widens to a track that descends to cross the dam of Llyn Croesor (mile 40·3), which supplied the quarry below.

- Continue straight ahead, leaving the lake behind you. The path is faint in places, and skirts the higher ground on the right. Eventually the slate tips of Rhosydd mine appear ahead and below.

Cwmorthin chapel

- Descend across the open, sometimes boggy hillside, aiming for a stile in front of a distinctive crag topped with a line of white quartz.

- Cross the stile and descend to Rhosydd mine workings. When you reach the main track running through the site, follow it to the right. The skeletal remains of the workers' barracks lie on your right.

- The track bears left between and below waste tips, going past the massive remains of a waterwheel on your left. Descend the steep track, which passes above the ruined workings of Conglog mine.

- Pass the remains of quarrymen's houses and the ruins of a chapel up on the right, with the lake, Llyn Cwmorthin, on the left. Cross the stream as it leaves the lake.

Llyn Cwmorthin

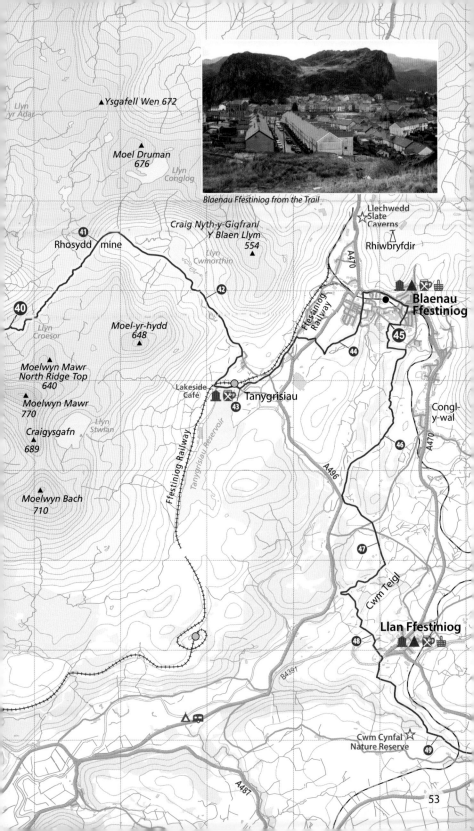

Blaenau Ffestiniog from the Trail

▲ Ysgafell Wen 672

Llyn yr Adar

▲ Moel Druman 676

Llyn Conglog

Craig Nyth-y-Gigfran/ Y Blaen Llym 554 ▲

Llyn Cwmorthin

Llechwedd ☆ Slate Caverns

⑪ Rhosydd mine

Rhiwbryfdir

④⓵

A470

④②

Ffestiniog Railway

Blaenau Ffestiniog

④⓪

Llyn Croesor

④④

④⑤

Moel-yr-hydd 648 ▲

Moelwyn Mawr North Ridge Top 640 ▲

Lakeside Café

Tanygrisiau

Congl-y-wal

Moelwyn Mawr 770 ▲

④③

④⑥

A470

Llyn Stwlan

Craigysgafn 689 ▲

Tanygrisiau Reservoir

A496

Ffestiniog Railway

Moelwyn Bach 710 ▲

④⑦

Cwm Teigl

Llan Ffestiniog

④⑧

B4391

④⑨

Cwm Cynfal Nature Reserve ☆

A487

Waterfall below Cwmorthin

- Descend the broad track, with the cascading river to your right. Go through the gate at the bottom to a parking area. When you reach Dolrhedyn Terrace, turn right to cross the stream and down to the bottom of the hill, over the Ffestiniog Railway to the Lakeside Café (mile 42·8).

- From the café, walk left along the road with Tanygrisiau reservoir on your right and the Ffestiniog Railway station on your left, until you reach a gap in the wall on your left.

- Go through it and follow the street through the quarry village of Tanygrisiau, bearing right down the hill at the junction.

- Pass the playing field and school on the right and continue straight ahead at the crossroads. Opposite number 1 Castell Barlwyd, turn in to the footpath on the right, and cross the river, past Afallon.

Lakeside Café, Tanygrisiau

- After the wooden stile, a faint and sometimes wet path passes through the field; note the slate washing-line post. This path, indistinct in places, tends right to another stile. Cross the stile, bearing left to another stile on the other side of the field.

- Cross the road and go up the lane ahead, which becomes a rough track. Pass between old buildings until you reach an abandoned cottage on your left. Turn sharp left and go through the gate almost immediately to the right.

- With the field boundary on your left, follow the path as it becomes enclosed by walls and squeezes between two old farm buildings. Continue on the footpath with a fence to the left and a wall to the right.

- Go through the metal gate and continue ahead down a shallow valley to follow the footpath and steps to Bryn Bowydd – a street with a row of cottages overlooking the valley.

- Continue into Dorvil Road, past Oakley Square and straight ahead, crossing the narrow footbridge over the Ffestiniog and mainline railways. Turn right along the High Street, noting the inscriptions on slate bands built into the pavements.

- Go along the High Street and, after passing the massive chisel-shaped sculptures in slate, turn right into Glynllifon Street. Pass over the disused railway, and go right again along Wynne Road.

- Immediately before the school (Ysgol y Moelwyn) on the left of Wynne Road, take the tarmac drive to reach the open hillside.

- Just before the school gate, follow the signed path to the left, and almost immediately fork right down wooden steps to a metal gate. Go left, steeply downhill, until you reach a lane and turn left.

- At the T-junction, go right and keep to the wide track, bearing right at the footpath sign. Then keep left until you meet a wide track coming from the left.

- Bear right again, and, at the next fork, leave the track and walk alongside the wall to your left. To your right, you will see opening views of the Moelwyn range and the Stwlan dam – the upper reservoir of the Tanygrisiau pumped storage hydroelectricity power station.

- Bear right again through a gap in the wall and then go left along the house drive. Go through the iron gate on your left next to the double footpath sign. Take the right hand path, cross a small stream and climb the hillside with the field boundary to your right.

Cwm Bowydd and Blaenau Ffestiniog

Cwm Teigl

- Ascending, cross a bridge of wooden railway sleepers. As a footpath joins from the left, keep to the right for a few metres, ignoring the gap in the wall, to follow the path leftwards and uphill, with the stone wall to your right.

- Cross the stone stile surmounted by crude ironwork and aim for the post in the field ahead. Bear left across the field to a kissing-gate in its far left corner. Cross the road and pass through the gate opposite.

- Continue ahead, cross the lane, then go over a stream to reach a gate beside a farm building. Go ahead along the farm track, with the drive of Pengwern Old Hall farm on your right.

- Reach a kissing-gate on your right and go through. Follow the path through the gorse to a metal gate leading to a clear path through the trees. It runs high above the Afon Teigl gorge so be aware of steep drops on your left.

- At the next path junction descend the right fork down steps to cross a wooden bridge, then climb up the far side of the valley. The soft path of pine needles leads to another sturdy wooden bridge.

- Before this bridge, turn sharp left along a path that takes you to a metal bridge over the Afon Teigl. Cross over, bearing right to a kissing-gate. At the derelict building, a walled track goes uphill: pass left through the metal gate and follow the track to the right through the field.

- Go through another gate and over a stile next to the farm. Before you reach the wall ahead, climb a stile on the right, and follow the narrow path through the woodland to a metal kissing-gate.

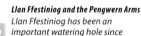

Llan Ffestiniog and the Pengwern Arms
Llan Ffestiniog has been an important watering hole since Roman times. It lies astride Sarn Helen, the Roman road that stretches from Canovium fort at Caerhun (Conwy valley) to the fort at Llandovery (near Brecon) – a distance of 160 miles/257 km. It passes through Tomen y Mur fort, near Llan Ffestiniog. The route was much used by drovers taking their animals to market and the Pengwern Arms was one of the major stopping places in the area. The Inn boasts a rich history and was visited by many travellers including George Borrow in 1854, while researching his book Wild Wales *(published in 1862)*

- Follow the path uphill between a wire fence and a narrow stream, through a gate and over a stile, to reach the road.

- Turn right and then left in front of a terrace of houses to reach the square beside the Pengwern Arms, a community-run pub. For some basic supplies, go up the road to the left for a few hundred metres and visit the small shop on your right.

3·5 Llan Ffestiniog to Penmachno

Distance	13·2 miles 21·3 km
Terrain	rough paths, open moorland with very boggy sections, quarry tracks
Grade	steep climb out of Cwm Cynfal, then steep descent into Cwm Penmachno followed by undulating forest walk into Penmachno
Food & drink	none between Llan Ffestiniog and Penmachno
Side trip	Rhiwbach quarry and village remains, Cwm Heritage Drop-in Room, St Tudclud`s church
Summary	a tough but rewarding day, from the spectacular gorge and waterfalls of the Afon Cynfal to open moorland and a taste of real wilderness, followed by a steep descent to the remote ruined village and quarry workings of Rhiwbach

	4·2	Llyn Morwynion	5·6	Cwm Penmachno	3·4	
Llan Ffestiniog	6·8		9·0		5·5	Penmachno

- From the Pengwern Arms, turn right down the road for just a few metres and cross over. Go through the gate into the field at the sign 'Rhaeadr Cynfal Falls'. Walk down the field to another gate on your left, signposted to the falls.

- Cross the field, aiming about 50 m left of the pole-mounted electricity substation, making for a footbridge in the bottom of the field. Climb the hill to a gate and along the path until you see two metal gates next to each other. Take the one on the right, signed 'Cynfal Falls'.

- Follow a broad grassy track alongside the wall/fence on your left, which takes you into the Cwm Cynfal Nature Reserve. Immediately turn right down the steps to the viewpoint. Cwm Cynfal is a hidden gem, little frequented but beautiful.

Cwm Cynfal

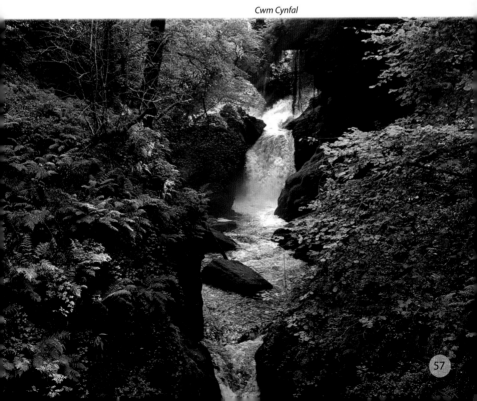

- After the viewpoint, turn right along a narrow path and follow the river upstream to join the main path. Descend this path down steps, cross the river and go up more steps to a path crossroads.
- Turn left at the crossroads, with the river to your left. This path hugs the edge of the gorge and is narrow in places. Exciting views may be enjoyed from the gorge edge, but take care.
- Pass under the towering viaduct, which carries the disused Blaenau Ffestiniog to Trawsfynydd railway. Continue up and down steps, through walls and over bridges, always with the rushing Afon Cynfal on your left.
- Cross a half-stile and turn right to reach a lane where you go left. At the road junction, bear left until you meet the main road (A470): beware of traffic. Go into the fields opposite over a stile located just behind the end of the bridge parapet.
- Follow the fence and the river on your left until you reach a wooden gate slightly up the slope. Skirt the steep bank on your left.
- The public footpath bears sharply left but this area can be boggy: to avoid the bog you may prefer to pass above four large boundary trees to reach a gap in the wall at the lower edge of the slope.
- Once through the gap, keep to the dilapidated wall on your left. Pass through a wooden gate into an area of reeds crossed by a clear path that leads to a stile into the woods.
- Go left along the forest track, passing an abandoned building on your left to reach a stream which the track crosses on an embankment. Before the stream, take the rough track that goes left to a sturdy wooden footbridge over the river. Cross the field, climbing to the gate at the top right corner.
- Turn right along the lane. At a fork, take the left track signed 'Fferm Cwm farm'. Just before this historic farm (see panel on page 59) go through the gate on the left into the field. Follow the wall and fence on your right, eventually to cross a stile. Afterwards, the route climbs left up the steep slope.
- Ascend a grassy path through the bracken, broadly along the field boundary and then beside a stream on your left. Near a small waterfall, bear right and continue with the fence on your left.

Cwm Cynfal near Cwm farm

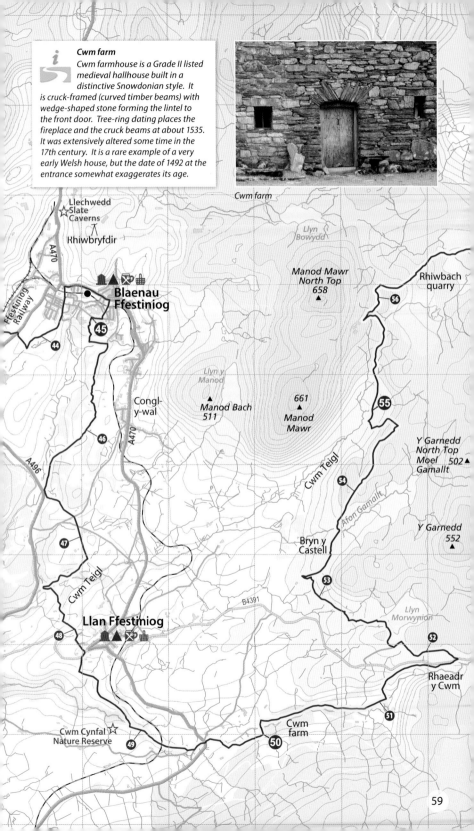

Cwm farm

Cwm farmhouse is a Grade II listed medieval hallhouse built in a distinctive Snowdonian style. It is cruck-framed (curved timber beams) with wedge-shaped stone forming the lintel to the front door. Tree-ring dating places the fireplace and the cruck beams at about 1535. It was extensively altered some time in the 17th century. It is a rare example of a very early Welsh house, but the date of 1492 at the entrance somewhat exaggerates its age.

Cwm farm

Llechwedd Slate Caverns

Rhiwbryfdir

A470

Ffestiniog Railway

Blaenau Ffestiniog

44

45

Congl-y-wal

A470

46

A496

Manod Mawr North Top 658 ▲

Llyn Bowydd

Rhiwbach quarry

56

Llyn y Manod

Manod Bach 511 ▲

661 ▲ Manod Mawr

55

Y Garnedd North Top Moel 502 ▲ Gamallt

Cwm Teigl

54

Afon Gamallt

Y Garnedd 552 ▲

47

Cwm Teigl

Bryn y Castell

53

B4391

Llyn Morwynion

Llan Ffestiniog

48

52

Rhaeadr y Cwm

Cwm Cynfal Nature Reserve

49

51

50 Cwm farm

- Pass a small slate tip and beware of a small mineshaft on the left, part of Cynfal copper mine. When you emerge onto fairly level ground, the view in front opens up to the impressive waterfall, Rhaeadr y Cwm.

- Ahead of you, the clear path contours the steep-sided valley, with the road above retained by high slate walls. Continue alongside the fence until you reach another gate to the road at a footpath sign. At the B4391, turn right and cross the road to the footpath sign just after the cattle grid.

- This next 5 km is the wildest of the entire Trail, much of it within the Migneint Site of Special Scientific Interest which features extensive dry heathland and blanket bog, mixed with seasonal ponds. Because waymarkers have had to be minimised, pay close attention to the map and instructions.

- Cross the stile and follow the fence, keeping to the slightly higher (and drier) ground to the right just below the crags. Aim for a stile in the left corner.

- The faint, grassy path beside the fence becomes a wider track, which passes over a hump between rocky outcrops.

- Follow the track to a T-junction and turn right towards Llyn Morwynion (Maidens' lake). ❶ Skirt the left end of the lake, cross the dam and look for an iron gate to the left at the junction of the fence and the wall. Pass through it, following a narrow path leftwards below the crags.

- At the footpath post just beyond a ruin, gradually descend the slope on the left to a galvanised gate in the wall ahead. Do not pass through this gate but instead continue with the wall on your left.

- Make your way through the rushes, ignoring a stile on your left. Contour the hillside on your right, keeping the wall to your left, until you reach a further stile a short way ahead.

- Cross the stile and follow faint sheep tracks to the left, keeping the fence on your left, until you reach the abandoned farmstead of Garreglwyd. Cross over the stile and skirt around the right of the farm until you reach a footpath sign.

- Cross the field as directed by the footpath sign. Keep to the left of a field enclosure, then skirt to the right of the marsh, aiming for a stile at the junction of a wall and a fence.

- Go over the stile. To the left are waterworks buildings. Scramble up the steep grassy hillside immediately in front of you to reach a broad grassy track.

- Turn right along this track, bearing left at all junctions. You may wish to make a short detour to the top of the hill on your left to visit Bryn y Castell ❷, a partly restored Iron Age fort.

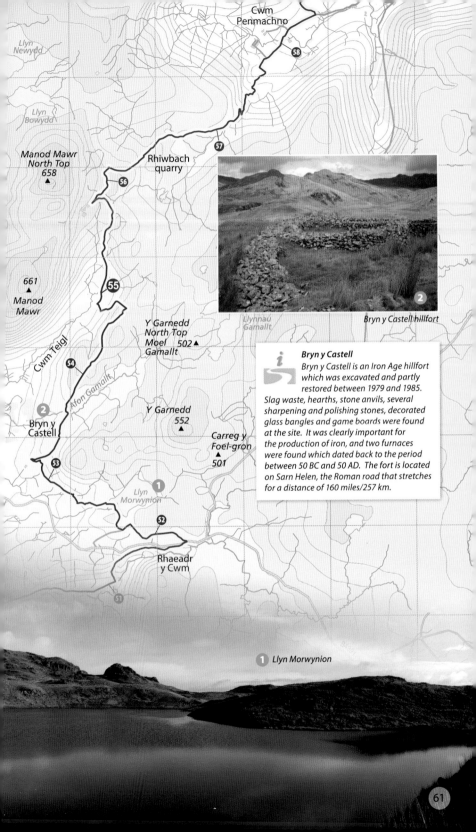

Cwm
Penmachno

58

Llyn
Newydd

57

Llyn
Bowydd

Manod Mawr
North Top
658 ▲

Rhiwbach
quarry

56

661 ▲
Manod
Mawr

55

Cwm Teigl

Y Garnedd
North Top
Moel   502 ▲
Gamallt

Afon Gamallt

54

2
Bryn y
Castell

Y Garnedd
552
▲

Carreg y
Foel-gron
▲
501

53

1
Llyn
Morwynion

52

Rhaeadr
y Cwm

51

Llynnau
Gamallt

Bryn y Castell hillfort

i Bryn y Castell

Bryn y Castell is an Iron Age hillfort which was excavated and partly restored between 1979 and 1985. Slag waste, hearths, stone anvils, several sharpening and polishing stones, decorated glass bangles and game boards were found at the site. It was clearly important for the production of iron, and two furnaces were found which dated back to the period between 50 BC and 50 AD. The fort is located on Sarn Helen, the Roman road that stretches for a distance of 160 miles/257 km.

1 Llyn Morwynion

- Follow the track leftwards into the valley of the Afon Gamallt, and cross it by a wooden footbridge. Continue along the track up the other side of the valley, beside the fence and along the line of Sarn Helen, the Roman road.
- Where the track bends off to the right, leave it to continue straight ahead, keeping to the fence past a small lake on its other side.
- Pass large rocky outcrops to left and right, along faint paths, where necessary taking to higher ground on the right to avoid wet areas, until you reach a footpath sign and stile.
- Cross the stile and descend the steep grassy slope as directed by the waymarker on the stile until you reach an old, grassy track going off left from the disused quarry. Take this, turning right when it reaches more level ground, to join the road at a prominent post.
- Climb the road to the right until you reach the quarry. At its entrance, go sharp right along a broad track which passes the remains of a radio station before dropping down to the Rhiwbach tramway (mile 56·1). This took slate from Rhiwbach quarry to Blaenau Ffestiniog, and it leads to the head of a steep incline.
- Go carefully down the steep incline, bearing slightly left towards a pond as the incline enters a cutting. Cross the stile and explore the ruins of the works and the village.
- When finished, follow the track to the right of the fence. The track veers right and passes between the remains of buildings before going steeply down between slate tips.

Cwm Teigl – the Trail runs along the near ridgeline

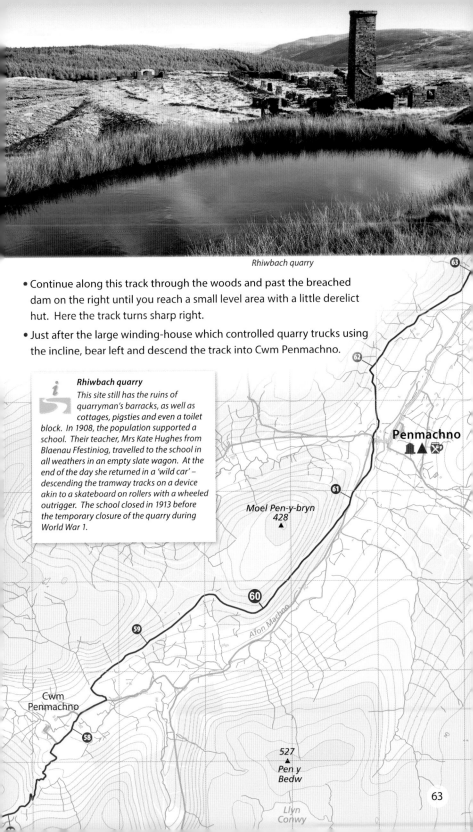

Rhiwbach quarry

- Continue along this track through the woods and past the breached dam on the right until you reach a small level area with a little derelict hut. Here the track turns sharp right.

- Just after the large winding-house which controlled quarry trucks using the incline, bear left and descend the track into Cwm Penmachno.

Rhiwbach quarry

This site still has the ruins of quarryman's barracks, as well as cottages, pigsties and even a toilet block. In 1908, the population supported a school. Their teacher, Mrs Kate Hughes from Blaenau Ffestiniog, travelled to the school in all weathers in an empty slate wagon. At the end of the day she returned in a 'wild car' – descending the tramway tracks on a device akin to a skateboard on rollers with a wheeled outrigger. The school closed in 1913 before the temporary closure of the quarry during World War 1.

Penmachno

Moel Pen-y-bryn
428

Cwm
Penmachno

527
Pen y
Bedw

Llyn
Conwy

Cwm Penmachno

- From the quarry gate, walk straight ahead along the road for about 770 m until you reach a converted church on the left. At this point, if time permits, visit the Cwm Heritage Drop-in Room about 50 m further down the road: access is gained on request and details of keyholders are given on the sign.

- Otherwise, go up the track on the left before the church. Climb the stile into the field and keep beside the fence, eventually to cross the stream on a timber footbridge.

- Follow a faint path up to a stile at the corner of the woods. Continue on the forest path, past the ruins of Hafod Fraith Uchaf. When you reach a forest road, turn right and follow it until you reach a forest crossroads.

- Continue straight ahead, and each time the track forks, bear right. After about 2·5 km you reach the road at the beginning of the Penmachno mountain bike trail.

- Turn left along the road for 175 m and then take the grassy lane down to the right, to pass stepping stones over the river. The grassy track becomes a tarmac road, White Street. At the fork, take the street on the left to reach Gethin Square outside the Eagles pub in the centre of Penmachno.

Penmachno

3·6 Penmachno to Capel Curig

Distance	11·2 miles 18·1 km
Terrain	undulating woodland, open moorland tracks and a length of improved riverside path
Grade	an easier day of gentle gradients on woodland, moorland and riverside paths
Food & drink	Tŷ Hyll, Capel Curig
Side trip	Cannon rocks (Betws-y-Coed), Tŷ Hyll (Ugly House)
Summary	a lovely and varied section combining the attractions of Swallow Falls, Miners' Bridge and Tŷ Hyll with wonderful views of Moel Siabod, the Carnedd and Glyder ranges from the moors above Capel Curig

```
        5·3          Betws-y-Coed          5·9
O────────────────────────O────────────────────────O
Penmachno  8·6                   9·5         Capel Curig
```

- From the Eagles pub, take the lane on the left of St Tudclud's church past Salem chapel. Cross the river past Tyn y Ddol, and go on up the hill to a sharp turn to the left.

- Leave the lane, and cross a stile ahead at the junction of the hedge and the fence. Go straight ahead up a faint path that becomes a track between the forest fence and an old stone wall, crossing a stile into the forest.

- Here, a narrow path bears left to reach the forest road. Follow this road to the right, keeping to the main track at the first fork. At a track T-junction, turn right again and continue to a lane.

- Turn right again onto this lane, and go over the river bridge. Look to the left to see the old packhorse bridge known as 'Roman Bridge', though it isn't Roman.

> **St Tudclud's church**
> St Tudclud's church is named after a 6th century saint, one of the five sons of Seithennyn who jointly ruled the Ancient Kingdom of Gwynedd with Maelgwn Gwynedd. The present church was built in 1859 and replaced a previous church from about 1600-20, itself a replacement for a 12th century church from which the font dates. The church has fine ancient Roman gravestones and a new stained glass window created by local artist, Yvonne Amor, together with village volunteers. After it closed in 1997, local people worked together to reopen the church in 2009.

Roman Bridge

65

- Pass Penmachno Mill on the right to reach the B4406. Turn left towards Conwy Falls Café. It is better to keep to the left-hand side of this sometimes busy road. **1**

- At the café, note the turquoise colour scheme of the Brondanw estate, last encountered in the Croesor valley. Go through the café car park to its far corner.

> Sir Clough Williams-Ellis
> 1883 - 1978
> Architect of Portmeirion
> Campaigner for the environment
> Designed Conwy Falls Café 1957

- Now follow the recently constructed permissive path through the woods. Its surface is rough with informal steps, and the path leads to broad woodland track above the Afon Conwy.

- Emerge from the woods to a view of Moel Siabod up the Lledr valley to the left. The path continues alongside fields and passes the Fairy Glen (£0.50 entrance charge) to reach the A470 trunk road. Cross the river, then immediately turn right onto a minor road.

- About 500 m after the railway bridge, take a track to the right at the footpath sign. Go through the woods and cross the railway by a bridge with high stone walls, then pass through the grounds of the Waterloo Hotel. From here, cross the road and look right for a good view of the magnificent 1815 Waterloo Bridge. **2**

- Follow the A5 left into the village of Betws-y-Coed, past the mini-market and over the Pont y Pair bridge on the right. Go immediately left towards the car park and along the Afon Llugwy on the wheelchair- and pushchair-friendly path, which starts opposite the toilet.

Waterloo Bridge **2**

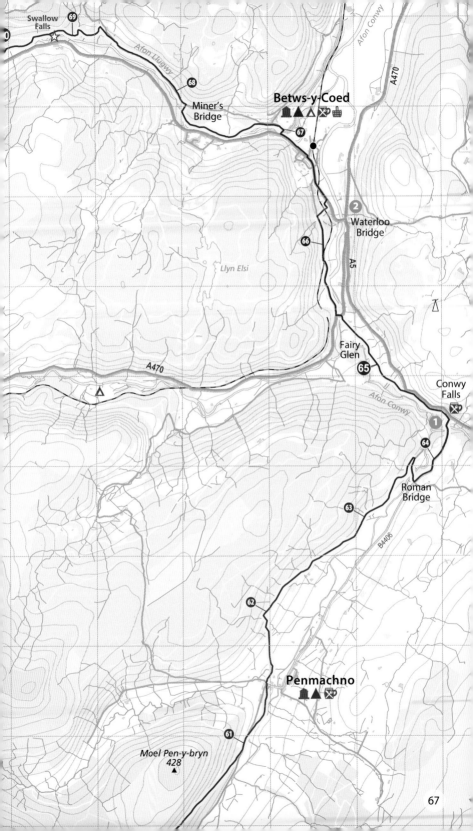

Swallow
Falls

Afon Llugwy

Miner's
Bridge

Betws-y-Coed

Afon Conwy

A470

A5

Waterloo
Bridge

Llyn Elsi

A470

Fairy
Glen

Conwy
Falls

Afon Conwy

Roman
Bridge

B4406

Penmachno

Moel Pen-y-bryn
428

- On the riverbank here can be seen cannon rocks, a local Victorian way of celebrating events by setting fire to channels and holes filled with gunpowder. At the end of the boardwalk, continue straight ahead, keeping to the river bank.

- Follow the river until you reach Miner's Bridge (mile 67·8) – a steeply sloping wooden bridge across the river down on your left. At this point, turn sharply right, ascending a steep slope through the woods to a minor road. The Trail continues to the left for about 1 km.

- At the footpath sign just before the road rises more steeply, enter the barriered forest road to the left. At the next junction, bear right. Where a further track comes in from the right, fork left and cross a timber bridge over the stream.

- The path descends steeply through the forest and passes through a derelict stone wall to join a good path coming in from the left. Turn right and after about 25 m, bear left.

Miner's Bridge

- Cross a second timber bridge, then follow a rough path under the trees. Eventually it goes beside a fence on a narrow ledge with steep cliffs above and below, to reach the spectacular Swallow Falls. Some say that the Welsh name 'Rhaeadr y Wennol' is a corruption of its original name, 'Rhaeadr Ewynnol' or foaming falls.

- Continue on the footpath and take the right fork, which becomes a forest road. After about 200 m, the Trail leaves the forest road on a path that descends to the left beside the river. Cross the stile into a field. Note the ruins of an old bridge across the river.

- The faint path follows the river, then a wall, before crossing a stile to the river bank. Climb the steps up to the A5 near Tŷ Hyll (Ugly House).

- After the car park on the right, ascend the very steep lane alongside Tŷ Hyll. After about 450 m, turn off sharp left along a forest road where the world-class Marin mountain bike trail crosses the lane. At the barrier to the forest road, fork left, keeping to the wall.

- At a bungalow, the forest road narrows to a path and, soon after, you cross a stile and a stream. Bear left below the slope and follow the fence on the left to pass another house.

- Climb another stile and ford a stream. The overgrown footpath runs beside a wall and joins a forest road. Turn left, ignoring a path and another forest road further on to the left.

> *i* **Tŷ Hyll**
> The 15th century cottage known as Tŷ Hyll (Ugly House) was said to have been built by two outlaw brothers. It is a 'Tŷ Un Nos' or One Night House. Under ancient Welsh law, anybody who completed a house between sunset and sunrise, with walls, roof and smoking chimney, could claim ownership of the building. An axe was then thrown and the freehold encompassed all the land within the circumference of the axe-throw. The house is now owned by the Snowdonia Society.

- About 70 m from the forest road junction, just before a sharp right bend, bear left along a wide grassy path. Cross a wooden bridge and continue on this path, sometimes wet, as it climbs steadily and becomes broad and grassy.

Tŷ Hyll

Tryfan from the Trail

- Join a forest road coming in from the right. Follow this road to the left, and keep left at a major track fork.

- Nearly 400 m after the fork, cross a stile in the wall junction. Go down an ancient sunken track between field boundaries and pick up a path into open moorland. The views open up ahead to the Glyder range, Moel Siabod and Snowdon.

- Go over a broad track and pass a large distinctive boulder. Cross the wooden bridge. When you reach three stiles in a cluster, stay on the main path through woods with a gate into open fields. The track, paved at first but later grassy, takes you over a stream and descends to Capel Curig at its climbing shop.

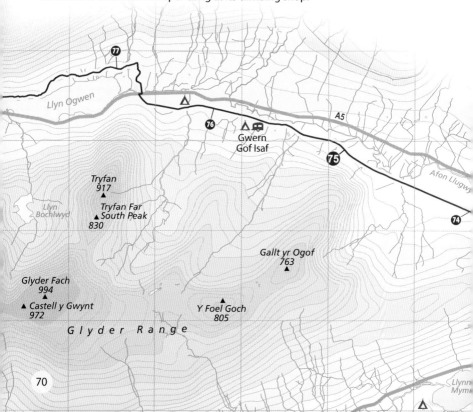

3·7 Capel Curig to Bethesda

Distance	**11·0 miles 17·6 km**
Terrain	**mountain tracks, narrow lanes and an off-road cycle path**
Grade	**an easy walk to Llyn Ogwen, then a rough path around the lake before a long downhill section and finally a level cycle path**
Side trip	**Llyn Idwal, Bont Ogwen carvings**
Food & drink	**Ogwen Cottage, Bethesda**
Summary	**the final section goes through the pass between the Carnedd and Glyder ranges; at Llyn Ogwen, the magnificent U-shaped valley of Nant Ffrancon opens up ahead and the finale is an easy walk round the blue slate tips of Penrhyn quarry**

	5·5	*Ogwen Cottage*	5·5	
Capel Curig	8·8		8·8	**Bethesda**

- Take the lane alongside the climbing shop, continue past the car park and go through a gate. Pick up a broad undulating track with the distinctive cone of Tryfan dominating the view ahead. This track goes all the way to Llyn Ogwen at the head of the Nant Ffrancon pass.

- When you reach the A5, cross the road and take the track opposite to the left, just a few metres further on. Pass the MAM climbing hut to Glan Dena farm entrance.

- Take the path to the right, cross a stile and follow the path beside Llyn Ogwen, waymarked by the National Trust.

- Eventually, after passing a solitary World War 2 gun shelter, you reach the dam at the end of the lake. After a 2-metre down and up scramble, the path arrives at the A5. Look under the river bridge to see the original coach-road bridge beneath it.

Llyn Idwal

This short but spectacular walk to the lake is only 1 km long but takes you into the heart of the mountains in the oldest National Nature Reserve in Wales. The ice-sculpted Cwm Idwal is surrounded by the towering crags of Glyder Fawr and Y Garn, while at its head is the deep gash of the Devil's Kitchen. The site is famous for its rock formations and its rare and fragile plant life, while the Idwal Slabs are a playground for climbers.

- From the stile in the wall, turn left to the cluster of buildings (including Ogwen Cottage outdoor centre, an exhibition room, toilet and a kiosk), then follow the narrow road for nearly 4·5 km. This was the original stagecoach road until Thomas Telford built the main road on the other side of the valley. The views are superb – back to the mountains and forward to the classic U-shaped valley of Nant Ffrancon.

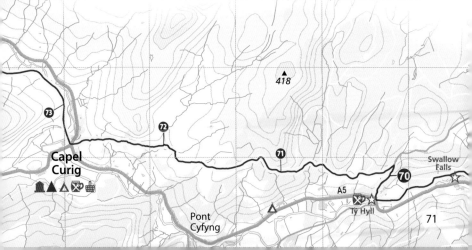

Rachub

A5
Ogwen

6

Bethesda

83

Penrhyn
Quarry

82

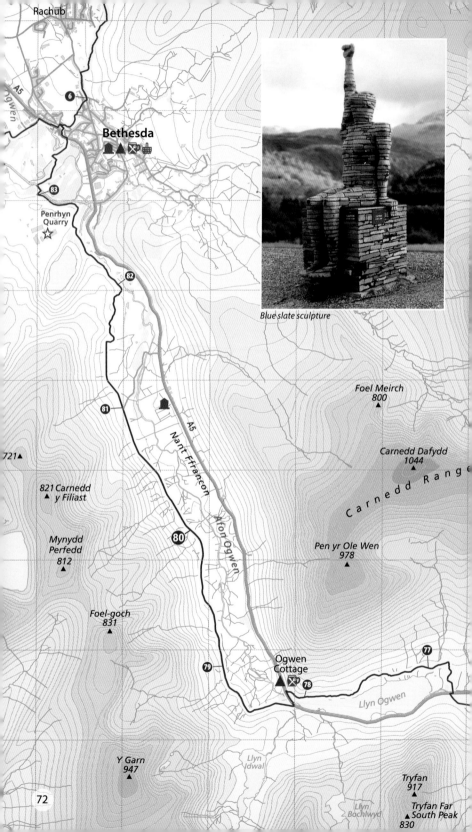
Blue slate sculpture

81

721▲

Foel Meirch
800
▲

Carnedd Dafydd
1044
▲

A5

Nant Ffrancon

821 Carnedd
▲ y Filiast

Carnedd Range

80

Afon Ogwen

Mynydd
Perfedd
812
▲

Pen yr Ole Wen
978
▲

Foel-goch
831
▲

77

79

Ogwen
Cottage
▲ ✕ 78

Llyn Ogwen

Y Garn
947
▲

Llyn
Idwal

Tryfan
917
▲

Tryfan Far
▲ South Peak
830

Llyn
Bochlwyd

72

- Where the road makes a sharp right bend, leave it to take the cycle track, Lôn Las Ogwen, straight ahead. The track meanders among and beside slate tips for a further 4 km. When you descend next to a bridge on the right, walk straight ahead. Take a look at the extensive historic graffiti on the bridge parapet.

- The track continues beside the river, crossing the Penrhyn quarry access road through two gates.

- The river here was diverted during the early days of slate mining into a deep gorge to allow slate extraction from the adjacent Penrhyn quarry. A little way up the access road is the impressive sculpture in blue slate of a seated man by Peter Barnes (near mile 82·5).

Statue at the end of the Trail

- After passing the derelict quarry hospital in the woods on your right, continue along the track which runs parallel to and above a road. At a signpost near some sheds and cottages down on the right, take a narrow path down to the right.

- At the road, turn left and then right along a paved track opposite cottage number 1. Bear right at a junction and keep the slate fence on your left.

- Pass the playing fields on your left, and cross the river to reach Bethesda High Street opposite the Seren Café. Turn left along the High Street until you reach an area of public art with a statue that marks the end of the Trail.

Congratulations! You have completed the Snowdonia Slate Trail and you can now catch the bus back to Bangor.

Nant Ffrancon valley

4 Reference

The Trail's origin and support

The Snowdonia Slate Trail was developed by Cwm Community Action Group to bring the unique slate culture and heritage to a wider audience, and to generate economic opportunities for the former slate villages. This guidebook has benefitted from financial support from the Heritage Lottery Fund and Magnox.

The official website for the Trail offers detailed information and updates on the path, as well as details of the 13 other contributors to the project: *www.snowdoniaslatetrail.org*.

Natural Resources Wales

This Welsh government-sponsored body employs 1900 staff and is responsible for protecting the natural resources and heritage of Wales. Its bilingual website is at *https://naturalresources.wales* and it endorses the Countryside Code as quoted on page 15.

Transport and travel

The nearest airports to the Trail are Manchester and Liverpool, served by several airlines within the UK and the rest of Europe including Ireland. For public transport details and timetables within and into Wales, in both English and Welsh, visit *www.traveline.cymru*. The Sherpa bus serves many parts of the Trail, although timings change with the season. For details, visit *www.gwynedd.llyw.cymru/en*.

Baggage transfer and guiding services

This is a new Trail but already some companies are offering baggage transfer and guiding services. Two of the first to make themselves known are:

RAW Adventures, which provides either guided or unguided services, supported by baggage transfer and accommodation booking. Contact them on 01286 870 870 or visit *www.raw-adventures.co.uk*.

Anelu/Aim Higher, which provides a fully guided service and can be contacted on 07877 902624 or visit *www.mountain-hill-courses.co.uk*. Further details on facilities are provided by *www.snowdoniaslatetrail.info* which will link to further support options as they emerge.

Visitor information

Details of tourist information offices are given on *www.visitsnowdonia.info*. This website can be searched by area, with links to accommodation and points of interest.

Hostels, campsites, budget accommodation

There are four youth hostels on or near the Trail: Llanberis, Snowdon Ranger (near Rhyd Ddu), Betws-y-Coed and Idwal (on Llyn Ogwen). For details, see *www.yha.org.uk*. Private hostels and bunk barns along the Trail include those at Bethesda, Dinorwig, Llanberis, Y Fron, Rhyd Ddu, Blaenau Ffestiniog, Llan Ffestiniog, Penmachno and Capel Curig. Campsites near or on the Trail are available at Llanberis, Waunfawr, Nantlle, Rhyd Ddu, Beddgelert, Betws-y-Coed and Capel Curig. Details of all of these can be found on *www.snowdoniaslatetrail.info*.

Maps: printed and online

Ordnance Survey Explorer maps at a scale of 1:25,000 cover the route area in two sheets: OL17 (Snowdon) and OL18 (Harlech, Porthmadog and Bala). However, the route of the Trail is not yet marked on these maps.

Please look at our detailed online route map at *www.rucsacs.com/routemap/sst* and zoom in for amazing detail on the route and its points of interest.

Further reading

Marshall, Des (2018) *Discovering Snowdonia`s Slate Heritage – 26 Great Walks* Kittiwake 978-1-908-748-52-2

Richards, Alun John (2001) *The Slate Railways of Wales* Gwasg Carreg Gwalch 0-8631-689-4

Richards, Alun John (2006) *Slate Quarrying in Wales* Gwasg Carreg Gwalch 1-84527-026-6

Avenue

London to P...

sustrans
JOIN THE MOVEMENT

2 Cathedral Square
College Green
Bristol
BS1 5DD
0117 926 8893
www.sustrans.org.uk

Second edition printed 2017

ISBN 978-1-910845-34-9

Whilst the authors have researched the routes for the purposes of this
guide, no responsibility can be accepted for any unforeseen circumstances
encountered whilst following them. The publisher would, however, welcome
any information regarding any material changes and any problems
encountered.

Front cover photo: Notre Dame, Paris
© Alex Hanoko, Creative Commons
Rear cover photo: Westminster and London Eye seen from Lambeth Bridge
© Richard Peace
Frontispiece: Traffic-free on the Avenue Verte near Neufchâtel-en-Bray
© Richard Peace

CONTENTS

INTRODUCTION...4

IN THE UK
159 km / 99 miles
LONDON - HORLEY 53 km / 33 miles...14
HORLEY - GROOMBRIDGE 39 km / 24 miles................................32
GROOMBRIDGE - NEWHAVEN 67 km / 42 miles...........................42

IN FRANCE

TO THE ROUTE SPLIT 82 km / 51 miles
DIEPPE - NEUFCHÂTEL-EN-BRAY 37 km / 23 miles.....................54
NEUFCHÂTEL-EN-BRAY - GOURNAY 45 km / 28 miles................64

WESTERN OPTION
120 km / 74 miles
GOURNAY - THE VEXIN 60 km / 37 miles....................................74
THE VEXIN - ST-GERMAIN 60 km / 37 miles...............................86

EASTERN OPTION
184 km / 114 miles
GOURNAY - BEAUVAIS 39 km / 24 miles.....................................96
BEAUVAIS - SENLIS 67 km / 42 miles..104
SENLIS - L'ISLE ADAM 37 km / 23 miles....................................114
L'ISLE ADAM - ST-GERMAIN 41 km / 25 miles............................122

AFTER THE ROUTE OPTIONS REJOIN
ST-GERMAIN - PARIS 37 km / 23 miles.......................................130

ROUTE TOTALS
WESTERN OPTION 398 KM 247 MILES
EASTERN OPTION 462 KM 287 MILES

The Avenue Verte - London to Paris by Bike

The route

Launched in summer 2012, the Avenue Verte cycle route connects two iconic sights, the London Eye and Notre Dame cathedral, letting you pedal between the hearts of both cities on traffic-free routes and quiet roads, taking in some fantastic landscapes along the way.

In England the route threads its way out of London on the leafy Wandle Trail before crossing the classic English countryside of the Downs and Weald, with their half-timbered villages and ancient churches. It then skirts south coast beaches, finally arriving at the Newhaven-Dieppe ferry.

In France, you pick up the superbly surfaced Pays de Bray Avenue Verte all the way to Forges-les-Eaux through the rolling rural Normandy countryside. The route then splits, the western option following a traffic-free path down the Epte valley before minor roads and tracks take you across the sleepy, rolling countryside of the Vexin, a protected regional park which cosies up to the edge of the greater Paris urban area.

The longer eastern option passes through the wonderful cathedral city of Beauvais and the splendidly ancient towns of Senlis and Chantilly, then heads over to the pretty river Oise for a final stretch along the river.

South of Dieppe

The route options rejoin for the final 60 km (40 miles) to Notre Dame, much of it traffic-free, along lovely sections of the River Seine, once the haunt of the Impressionist painters. In Paris itself you follow cycle paths along the Saint-Denis and Saint-Martin canals before cycling along quiet streets to the river Seine and France's most revered and famous building, Notre Dame cathedral. Note there are 'short cut' options not part of the official Avenue Verte route (pages 29-37 and pages 144-149) and also a spur to Giverney to visit Monet's garden.

Background

The Avenue Verte project has involved East Sussex, West Sussex and Surrey County Councils, Transport for London (TfL) and Sustrans, in partnership with the Département de Seine-Maritime in France.

The idea for this iconic route had long been planned on both sides of the channel, but the catalyst came with the 2012 London Olympics which seemed an opportune moment to turn plans into reality.

Whilst the initial route contains some sections that are of interim standard, the route retains its initial stated aims of creating an 'alternative, car-free, gentler route between London and Paris for walkers and cyclists and especially for families.'

The route will continue to be developed on the French side especially, to include more traffic-free sections and greenways. For example this new second edition contains details of a recent traffic-free trail between Gournay and Beauvais.

Sustrans and the National Cycle Network

 Sustrans is the charity making it easier for people to walk and cycle. They are behind many groundbreaking projects including the National Cycle Network, over 14,000 miles of signed cycling and walking routes on traffic-free paths and quiet roads across the UK.

Created from one of the first ever National Lottery grants in 1995, the popularity of the Network has grown enormously and it now carries over a million walking and cycling journeys daily and passes within a mile of 57% of the population (for examples of signs you will see when cycling on the National Cycle Network see overleaf).

The maintenance and the development of the National Cycle Network and Sustrans' other projects rely on the kind donations of Sustrans supporters. **Make your move and support Sustrans today!** Visit www.sustrans.org.uk or call 0300 303 2604 to find out more.

Route surface and signage

Most of the route shown in green on the following maps is traffic-free and suitable for new and returning cyclists and families.

There are some short sections of the route that use bridleways where the route surface is variable and can be rough; these are not suitable for road bikes (they are mainly on the western route option in France as it crosses the Vexin). There are on-road route alternatives here though.

At the time of writing around 40% of the route is traffic-free. The traffic-free proportion will increase over time.

The Avenue Verte uses a mix of established National Cycle Network routes 2, 4, 20 and 21 as follows:

Route	From	To
NCN 4	London Eye	Chelsea Bridge
NCN 20	Wandle Trail at Earlsfield	Merstham, north of Redhill
NCN 21	Merstham	Crawley
NCN 20	Crawley	Crawley
NCN 21	Crawley	Polegate
NCN 2	Polegate	Newhaven

Note that Avenue Verte logos may only be provided intermittently on some sections and are often provided as 'patch' signs on existing, larger NCN signs but you will have the reassurance of more continuous NCN signing in between.

The Avenue Verte also follows sections of local route in London: Cycle Superhighway 8 very briefly across Chelsea Bridge and past Battersea Park, and London Cycle Network Routes 5 then 3 from Battersea Park up to Clapham and Wandsworth Commons then joining NCN 20, the Wandle Trail, near Earlsfield train station. There is also a local route link between NCN 20 and 21 in Crawley.

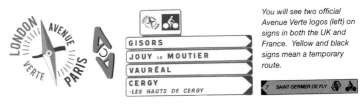

You will see two official Avenue Verte logos (left) on signs in both the UK and France. Yellow and black signs mean a temporary route.

Avenue Verte logos will often appear together with National Cycle Network signs (right)

In France the full Avenue Verte logo signing appears more often along with the widespread green and white cycle route signing that can be found in many places across the country. Signs for temporary sections of the Avenue Verte are yellow, as above. Until 2012 France lacked a plan for a national signing system and green and white signage will probably remain the most frequently encountered type for some time to come, but there are also many local variants. However, a programme is starting to standardise French cycle signage, creating a national network from the many fine routes that already exist on the ground and which will be added to in future.

Eurovelo routes are those which run across European boundaries and bear the familiar yellow stars on blue background logo. National routes within France will be designated as *Véloroutes* and have their own consistent signage. The system however, is in its infancy.

How long does it take?

This guide splits the route into chapters each based around a reasonably comfortable day's ride, with the western option comprising eight days riding and ten days on the eastern. These are based on distances an average leisure rider would find comfortable. Allow extra riding time for the urban sections at either end as they involve more complex navigation and present a plethora of sightseeing opportunities.

If you want to tackle slightly bigger daily mileages the western option is easily squeezed down into a week by combining the first two days' riding in France, going straight from Dieppe to Gournay, as some 47 km (29 miles) of this 82 km (51 miles) section are on a superb, fast, traffic-free tarmac path. Tackling the eastern option in seven days is a bit more of a challenge but a sensible option could be achieved by going straight from Dieppe to Gournay in a single day's ride with subsequent days as follows:

Gournay to Senlis 106 km (66 miles)
Senlis to Conflans-Sainte-Honorine 66 km (38 miles)
Conflans-Sainte-Honorine to Paris 58 km (33 miles)

Further information online

www.francevelotourisme.com
A new French organisation promoting use of the developing network of long distance cycle routes, and a very useful source of English language information about the route, including maps, stage information and accommodation.

www.avenuevertelondonparis.com
This dedicated website has been put together in French and English. There are wonderful, detailed zoomable route maps showing accommodation options and many other services as well as lots of advice on the practicalities of tackling the route.

www.sustrans.org.uk
Founders of the UK's National Cycle Network and charitable campaigners for sustainable transport in general. See page 5 for more information.

www.eurovelo.com
EuroVelo is the European cycle route network. It is a project of the European Cyclists' Federation (ECF) that aims to develop a network of high-quality cycling routes that connect the whole continent.

www.normandy-tourism.org/cycling
Cycling specific information for Normandy

Practical Information

Preparing for the ride
Before you go, check your bike is in good condition - make sure the tyres are pumped up and the seat and handlebars are set to the right position. Also check brakes and lights are in good order and tightly secured, gears are changing smoothly, and gear and brake cables aren't rusty or frayed. Wheel quick releases should be in the closed position and the chain should be clean and lubricated.

What to wear
You shouldn't need to invest in lots of specialist clothing or footwear to enjoy the Avenue Verte. Wear thin layers which you can easily add or remove as you go, and choose light, breathable fabrics. Take a waterproof, hat and gloves (your extremities are more exposed when cycling), and if you're going to be cycling at night, take a bright, reflective top. Padded shorts can be helpful for extra comfort when riding too.

Useful kit list
- Puncture repair kit & pump
- Tyre levers & spare inner tubes
- Water bottle
- Bike oil or lubricant
- Bike lights
- Bike 'multi-tool' or Allen keys & adjustable spanner
- Bike lock, bungee cords & panniers to carry luggage

Bike accessories
A bike bell is a must for any cyclist as it lets you warn pedestrians of your approach. Wearing a helmet is not compulsory in France or England so the decision is ultimately a question of individual choice – however although helmets can't prevent accidents from happening they can protect you if they do occur and are especially recommended for young children.

Comfortable clothing and a hybrid bike are ideal for exploring the Avenue Verte.

Even in central Paris there are cycle lanes safe enough for children. Here is the Avenue Verte at Bassin de la Villette.

Cycling with children

The Avenue Verte is generally easygoing cycling and even when you do pass through hills the gradients tend to be reasonably gentle. It also has a good amount of traffic-free riding, all of which make it well suited to cycling with children.

If cycling with a family, remember to keep children in front of you on roads (or in between if there are two of you), and take special care at road junctions. Plan day stages carefully with plenty of refreshment stops, and remember to keep toddlers wrapped up so they don't lose heat when you're pedalling.

What kind of bike?

The best bike to tackle the Avenue Verte on is a hybrid bike, rather than a racer, due to the small sections with a rough surface. However you can use any bike.

Good cycling code

- Always follow the Highway Code, or French Code de la Route
- Cycle at a safe and responsible speed
- Give way to pedestrians
- Remember that some people are hard of hearing and visually impaired. Don't assume they can see or hear you
- Where there are wheelchair users or horse riders please give way
- Ring a bell or call out to warn of your approach – acknowledge people who give way to you
- Follow the Countryside Code; in particular respect crops, livestock and wildlife and take litter home
- Take special care at junctions, when cycling downhill and on loose surfaces
- Always carry food, water, a puncture repair kit, a map and waterproofs
- Keep your bike roadworthy; use lights in poor visibility
- Consider wearing a helmet and high visibility clothing

Cycling in France

It is simply a pleasure. France is a cycling nation and accords cyclists status on the road and some great facilities, from wonderful off-road riding to city centre automated bike hire. If you're unfamiliar with cycling in France here are a few handy tips.

You will no doubt know to ride on the right hand side of the road, path or track you are on. However, there is an old rule of the road called priority from the right which is still a consideration. In the absence of all other signs this rule still applies - it means traffic joining from the right has priority - even if on a seemingly minor road. If, though, your road has yellow diamonds on white background signs you have priority, until you come to one with a black line through. Side roads often have stop or give way markings and roundabouts also usually have give way systems so this rule won't apply here. However, this is not always so, and in any case it's wise to make a habit of treating traffic coming from the right with extra caution as some drivers may still adhere to the old law!

In France traffic lights go directly from red to green but do go to amber between green and red. A red light accompanied by an amber flashing arrow pointing to the right means you can turn right as long as you give way to other vehicles. A green light replaced by a flashing yellow light means you may proceed but have to give way to crossing traffic and pedestrians.

Where a cycle path is indicated by a white bicycle on a circular blue background, it is obligatory to use it in preference to the road. Where it is on a rectangular background, it is optional.

Parisian cycle lanes; keep to the right.

Travel information

Bikes on UK trains

Bikes are carried free of charge on most UK trains, but spaces are usually limited and reservations are sometimes required, especially on intercity services. You can reserve a space for your bike when you book or by calling the train operator. There are normally no restrictions on folding bikes. For full UK travel information visit **www.nationalrail.co.uk** or call 03457 48 49 50

Eurostar

You have three options for taking bikes on Eurostar:
1. Full sized bikes taken on the same train as you. These must be booked in advance (i.e. at the same time as booking your ticket) and cost £30 per bike one way. Allow time before boarding to take it to the baggage office, a little distance from the boarding area at both London St Pancras International and Paris Gare du Nord.
2. As registered luggage, travelling on a separate train to passengers and arriving within 24 hours of the passenger. Bagged bikes of length 85-120cm cost £10 per bike. The costs rises to £25 per bike if the bagged bike is over 120cm long or if fully assembled and not bagged. This service can be booked on the day of travel. Note tandems are not allowed.
3. As hand luggage on the train with you. The bike must be bagged and not more than 85cm in length (in practice this usually means small folders only). Eurostar is at **www.eurostar.com** or telephone 03448 225 822.

French train operators

French railways (SNCF) will carry, free and as normal luggage, folding bikes or bagged, dismantled bikes to a maximum of 120cm x 90cm.

Many French trains will carry fully assembled bikes. This service is generally free of charge but on TGV high-speed trains bike spaces, if available, must be booked in advance.

Along the Avenue Verte you may want to make particular use of trains in and around Paris and express trains are great for getting your bike into and out of central Paris in one short hop:

(RER) (A) RER services are recognisable by an RER logo plus line logo and there are five lines, A to E, operating in the greater Paris area. **www.ratp.fr/en**

Transilien services run within the Île de France area and, like RER services, carry bikes outside of morning and evening rush hours.

French rail tickets can be booked online from the UK - Rail Europe can give you details of the current system of doing this and can also sell you your train tickets direct.

www.sncf.com is the website for French trains. **www.sncf.co.uk** and **Rail Europe** is now branded as **voyages-sncf.com** and can be telephoned on 0844 8485848.

Ferry

Going as a foot passenger between Newhaven and Dieppe you usually have to board with the motor vehicles and lash your bike to the deck side or elsewhere as directed by crew. When booking you should include your bike (which needs booking on even if there's no charge for it; bike space is limited). Transmanche run two ferry crossings a day (plus possible summer evening sailing) from Newhaven to Dieppe (and vice versa), taking around four hours. For more information visit **www.transmanche.co.uk** or call 0844 493 0651

European Bike Express

This is easy and efficient travel specifically for cyclists. Stops in Northern France include Calais, St-Witz north of Paris (so handy for a UK return after cycling the Avenue Verte - take RER line D to Survilliers Fosses and St-Witz is about 2.5 km / 1.5 miles from here), Thionville, Nancy, Nemours and Auxerre. Their air conditioned coaches have reclining seats and pull a purpose-built trailer capable of carrying bikes and bike trailers. Runs throughout the summer serving western France on an Atlantic route and central, Alpine and Mediterranean France (and even into Spain) on other routes. Single or return journeys. UK pick-up points down the eastern side of England between North Yorkshire and Kent, with an M62 / M6 feeder service on certain dates.
www.bike-express.co.uk
3, Newfield Lane, South Cave. HU15 2JW   01430 422111

Travel in style between Newhaven and Dieppe

The tall narrow apartments of many Paris districts can make finding cycle friendly hotels tricky.

Accommodation listings and contacts

The listings in the guide shown with blue numbering **1** have been chosen because they are both near the route, not too highly priced and usually quite near the beginning or end of the day sections.

This is of course just a cross-section of what is available and by travelling a little further off the route plenty more accommodation opportunities open up. Several national organisations also offer accommodation or listings services:

UK

Beds for Cyclists **www.bedsforcyclists.co.uk**
Camping and Caravanning Club **www.campingandcaravanningclub.co.uk**
Visit Britain **www.visitbritain.com**
Youth Hostels Association **www.yha.org.uk**
Independent Hostel Guide **www.independenthostels.co.uk**

France

France Velo Tourisme **www.francevelotourisme.com**
FVT manage the Accueil Vélo (Cyclists Welcome) scheme. Details of providers are shown on route maps with a green logo as right. Accueil Vélo accreditation should guarantee secure bike storage and a repair kit. Many also provide cycling information on local cycle routes and a hearty breakfast. We have tried to insure that all other guide accommodation entries are cycle-friendly but please double check before booking.
FUAJ (French YHA equivalent) **www.fuaj.org**
Avenue Verte official website **www.avenuevertelondonparis.com**
Good accommodation section at **www.freewheelingfrance.com**

The Avenue Verte start is
across the bridge from
Westminster

London ~ Horley

Your start is the River Thames; 'liquid history' as one writer on London called it. The route start at the London Eye means you get the chance to survey one of the most famous views in the world, along the river from Westminster Bridge. You are soon threading your way through the heart of London, then across the green expanses of Clapham and Wandsworth Commons, busy with relaxing Londoners at weekends, before escaping motor traffic completely along the leafy Wandle Trail. Quiet minor roads lead over the beautiful, gentle North Downs.

Route Info

Distance 53 kilometres / 33 miles
Note Chaldon / Crawley Down shortcut is overall 8 miles shorter (pages 28-31 & 37)

Terrain & Route Surface After negotiating some traffic in central London you soon find yourself on the tarmac cyclepaths over Clapham and Wandsworth Commons. Join the Wandle Trail near Earlsfield train station, which has a variety of surfaces, from tarmac to earth paths that may get muddy after rain.
The trail gradients are easy and there are plenty of refreshment stops en route. Leaving the trail at Carshalton, you are mainly on minor suburban roads, now encountering your first real hills, before a lovely minor road crossing of the North Downs. The easy pedalling final section uses a series of beautiful tiny roads and tracks through Nutfield Marsh to Redhill centre before minor roads, tracks and cycle lanes lead to Horley.

Off-road 31% traffic-free on a variety of surfaces but often tarmac or good quality crushed stone. You will encounter bumpy stone and possibly mud on the Worth and Forest Ways, especially approaching Groombridge.

Profile

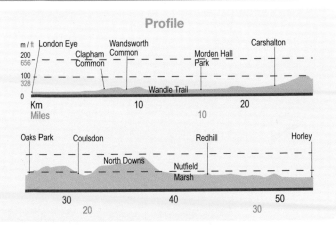

15

What to See & Do

• **Cycling** is a growing trend in London and the ever-expanding **National Cycle Network** in the capital has played its part, along with such developments as public hire bikes ('Boris bikes' after the former mayor of London). There are plenty of green, traffic-free escapes suitable for family cycling in the heart of the city, whether it's a cross-town jaunt on the Regent's Canal, a spin around Hyde Park or an exploration of East London along the Greenway.

• **Westminster** is much more than the Houses of Parliament and the Abbey; the area around the start of the Avenue Verte holds plenty of hidden treasures too. Seek out **Victoria Tower Gardens** by the south-west corner of the Houses of Parliament, a lovely green space with great views and an interesting mix of sculptures and monuments. To the west of these gardens lies a picturesque maze of quiet streets clustered around Smith Square.

• It's a fine traffic-free ride along the **Chelsea Embankment**, from the Chelsea Bridge to Albert Bridge. This is easily combined with a spin around **Battersea Park** with its children's zoo, boating lake and Peace Pagoda.

• Although the Avenue Verte heads west from Westminster Bridge, **National Cycle Network Route 4** is a great way to explore the Thames' attractions to the east. These include Tower Bridge, the Cutty Sark, Greenwich Park and the Thames Barrier. There are also the remarkable Cycle Superhighways which are well worth exploring; in fact this chapter suggests using CS8 to Chelsea Bridge as a quicker, largely traffic-free alternative to the official route.

• The **Garden Museum** is in a former church next to Lambeth Palace, with a range of exhibits relating to everything from royal gardens to small backyards. It's also the last resting place of 17th century gardeners and planthunters John and John Tradescant, father and son. Recent multi-million pound expansion. Includes cafe.

Cycle Superhighway 8 (CS8)

• It's a splendid ride on a nice tarmac path over **Clapham Common**, passing the wonderful Italian cafe La Baita. There are also eating opportunities as you cross lovely **Wandsworth Common**.

• **The Wandle Trail** is a cycling and walking route following the river Wandle from Wandsworth, where it flows into the Thames, to Carshalton 15 km (9 miles) upstream at the river source. Once more than 90 mills lined its banks, making the River Wandle the most industrial in England. Today, parks largely replace the industry, and are the basis of NCN 20 in London.

• **Wimbledon** boasts the history of tennis at the Wimbledon Lawn Tennis Museum (www.wimbledon.com) and local heritage at Wimbledon Windmill Museum. **Merton Abbey Mills** craft village nearby has plenty of eateries.

• **Deen City Farm** is a community project with riding stables, pet farm and good priced cafe. www.deencityfarm.co.uk

• The National Trust Property at **Morden Hall** is well worth putting aside time for; it combines 125 acres

of lovely parkland and its distinctive and characterful footbridges with the imposing hall itself, as well as preserved watermills (where tobacco was once ground), Morden cottage and a huge variety of landscapes, from rose gardens to marshland. A choice of cafes awaits too. www.nationaltrust.org.uk

• It's hard to believe that **Farthing Down**, crossed by the Avenue Verte along Ditches Lane, is still within Greater London. These North Downs chalk grasslands are a Site of Special Scientific Interest. You also pass through pretty Chaldon with a centuries old mural in the church.

• **Mercers Park**, by the route north of Redhill, is noted for the interesting bird population and watersports.

• The splendid landscaped grounds of **Gatton Park** lie to the north of Redhill and make a fine bike ride. www.gattonpark.com

• Historic **Reigate** lies about 2.5 km (1.5) miles west of the Avenue Verte as it passes through Redhill. Attractions include a conservation area, Priory Park and windmills.

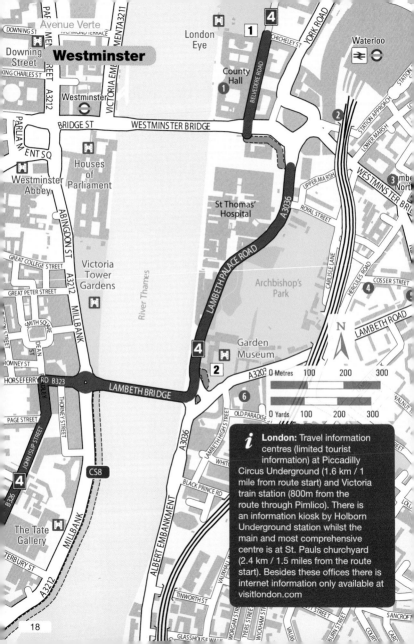

Westminster

i **London:** Travel information centres (limited tourist information) at Piccadilly Circus Underground (1.6 km / 1 mile from route start) and Victoria train station (800m from the route through Pimlico). There is an information kiosk by Holborn Underground station whilst the main and most comprehensive centre is at St. Pauls churchyard (2.4 km / 1.5 miles from the route start). Besides these offices there is internet information only available at visitlondon.com

Directions

1 The route begins outside the iconic London Eye – the first of many landmarks you will see on your journey to Paris along the Avenue Verte. Set off on Belvedere Road and head south until the junction with Westminster Bridge, cross the road on the toucan crossing, then turn L onto the shared use pavement and follow the road around to the R. Cross Lambeth Palace Road using the toucan crossing and rejoin the road, heading along the cycle lane. NB From Westminster to Chelsea Bridge follow NCN 4 signs.

2 At the roundabout at Lambeth Bridge head into the 'channelled' cycle lane in the middle of the road then across the bridge. On the other side, head straight over the roundabout, and take the second L onto Dean Ryle Street. Continue straight on to John Islip Street. **Note:** At Lambeth Bridge there is a quicker (non-Avenue Verte) alternative; L immediately over Lambeth Bridge onto Cycle Superhighway 8. Follow the excellent blue cycleway past Vauxhall Bridge, to the Avenue Verte at Chelsea Bridge.

Victoria Tower Gardens

Accommodation

1 PREMIER INN
London County Hall, Belvedere Road SE1 7PB
0871 5278648   www.premierinn.com

2 THE WALRUS BAR AND HOSTEL
172, Westminster Bridge Road SE1 7RW
020 7928 4368 thewalrusbarandhostel.com
Mainly mixed-sex dormitory style accommodation

3 TUNE HOTEL
118-120 Westminster Bridge Road SE1 7RW
020 7633 9317   tunehotels.com

4 THE STEAM ENGINE
41-42, Cosser Street SE1 7BU   020 79280720
www.publovehostels.co.uk Mixed dormitories

5 DAYS HOTEL LONDON WATERLOO
54, Kennington Road SE1 7BJ
020 7922 1331   www.daysinn.co.uk

6 NOVOTEL
113 Lambeth Road SE1 7LS
020 7660 0674 novotel.com

OTHER LONDON ACCOMMODATION
YHA Hostels nearest route start are St. Paul's and Oxford Street, both just over 2 km away. Neither has a cycle store. St. Pancras about 3.5 km away has cycle store, as do Earl's Court and Thameside, each about 5.5 km away.
Dover Castle Hostel 6A, Great Dover Street, Borough SE1 4 XW 020 7403 7773
dovercastlehostel.com Mixed dorms. 2 km away.

A CRYSTAL PALACE CARAVAN CLUB SITE
Crystal Palace Parade SE19 1UF 020 8778 7155
www.caravanclub.co.uk   Non-members and tent campers welcome. Tent pitches May to Sept. 8 km (5 miles) east of the route as it passes through Wimbledon.

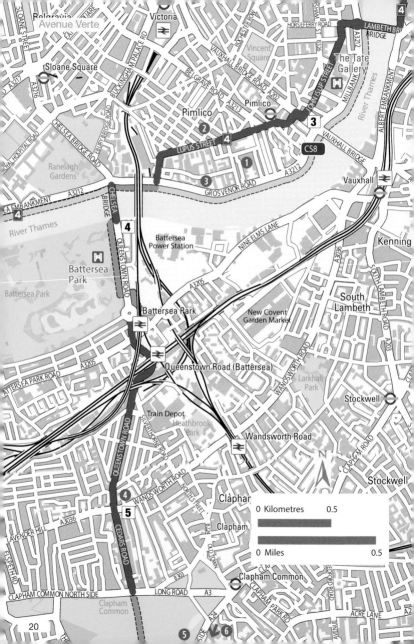

3 At the end of John Islip Street turn R onto Vauxhall Bridge Road, then immediate L onto Drummond Gate using the slip road. When the road forks, continue straight on into Lupus Street. Follow the road for its length, curving L, and when you reach the river turn R onto Cycle Superhighway 8. Continue to the junction with Chelsea Bridge, rejoin the road and turn L onto this beautiful bridge.

4 Once on the other side, continue straight on along Queenstown Road (still on Cycle Superhighway 8). At the roundabout head straight on (second exit) - cycle the roundabout or use the segregated cycle lane around the edge before rejoining the road. Continue straight over the junction and follow Queenstown Road for its full length (**take care - busy at rush hour**).

5 Continue straight onto Cedars Road until you reach Clapham Common, where the route heads straight into the park at the traffic lights. Join the cycle path over the Common. Keep an eye out for the recenty restored Victorian bandstand on your R.

❶ DOLPHIN HOUSE
Chichester Street, Dolphin Square SW1V 3LX
020 78343800 dolphinsquare.co.uk

❷ ST GEORGES PIMLICO
115 St Georges Drive SW1V 4DA
020 78340210 stgeorgespimlico.com

❸ TRAVEL JOY HOSTELS
111 Grovesnor Road SW1V 3LG
020 78349689 traveljoyhostels.com

❹ PREMIER INN WANDSWORTH ROAD
638-640 Wandsworth Road SW8 3JW
0871 5279678 premierinn.com

❺ THE WINDMILL
Clapham Common South Side SW4 9DE
020 86734578 windmillclapham.co.uk

❻ EUROHOTEL / EUROLODGE
Both on Clapham Common South Side
020 86733534 / 020 87721234 eurohotelslondon.co.uk

Rail stations are along virtually the whole route to Horley, itself around 45 minutes from London Bridge or London Victoria. Stations are serviced by the following companies whose bikes on trains policies are described (note folding bikes generally carried on all services free of charge):

Southern Bikes free of charge. Reservations not required. Restrictions Mon - Fri:
• 7-10 am on any train due to arrive into London
• 4-7 pm on trains due to depart from London.
03451 27 29 20 www.southernrailway.com

Thameslink
Bikes free of charge. Reservations not required. Restrictions Mon-Fri:
• On trains travelling towards London south of Luton Airport Parkway passing through or arriving at any central London station between 7-10 am
• On trains departing London and passing through or stopping at any central London station between 4-7 pm.
0345 026 4700 www.thameslinkrailway.com

Gatwick Express Bikes free of charge. Reservations not required. Two cycle spaces per train.
Restrictions Mon - Fri:
• 7-10 am on any train due to arrive into London Victoria
• 4-7 pm on any train due to depart from London Victoria.
0345 850 1530 www.gatwickexpress.com

London Underground Folded bikes are allowed on anywhere, any time.
Non-folders allowed on some lines, free of charge, but not between 7.30-9.30 am and 4-7 pm. The most useful of these for accessing the Avenue Verte is the District Line, which has several stations on or near the route, including Westminster, Victoria and Wimbledon. For full details including a downloadable PDF 'bikes on the tube' map see www.tfl.gov.uk

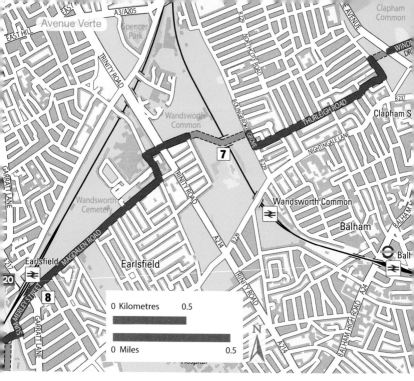

6 On the south side of Clapham Common turn R onto Windmill Drive, cross The Avenue, then follow the path west through the park until you reach Clapham Common West Side, where you'll need to turn L. Head along the cycle cut-through and turn R, onto Thurleigh Road. At the end turn right onto Bolingbroke Grove. At the crossing, where the route turns left into Wandsworth Common, go onto the segregated path. Follow this until you reach the bridge over the railway lines.

7 On the other side of the railway take the path stretching diagonally across the Common to Dorlcote Road. Follow this road and cross Trinity Road using the toucan crossing, and head straight on, onto Alma Terrace. Turn L onto Lyford Road then R onto Magdalen Road at the mini roundabout.

8 Follow this road until you reach Garratt Lane at the traffic lights, where you turn L (a permitted movement for cycles only). Once on the high street take an immediate R turn onto Summerley Street (take care high street often quite busy).

9 Follow Summerley Street south, and turn R at the end onto Trewint Street, a narrow road that leads onto a bridge over the River Wandle. From here follow signs for the Wandle Trail / NCN20. On the other side of the bridge turn L onto the riverside path and follow it south.

Clapham Common

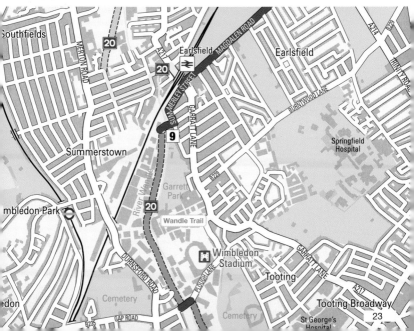

23

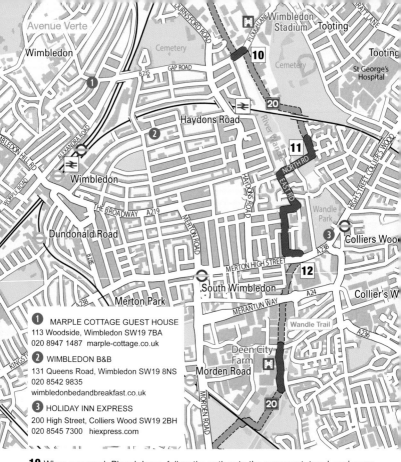

10 When you reach Plough Lane, follow the path onto the pavement, turn L and cross using the toucan crossing, before continuing south onto the riverside path.

11 At the southern end of the path head straight on to Chaucer Way. Follow it until you reach the junction with North Road, turn R and head across the bridge. Continue straight on to the mini roundabout. Turn L down East Road.

When you reach the width restriction turn R onto All Saints Road, and then L onto Hanover Road. Follow this until you see the dead end, and turn L into Holmes Road.

12 Cross Merton High Street using the toucan crossing. On the other side turn R onto the traffic-free path. When the path ends, cross the car park and head through the stone arch to the toucan crossing over Merantun Way. Cross over the road and join the traffic-free path straight ahead. The ruins of Merton Abbey are located just to the east of the path, as is Merton Abbey Mills with a market and cafe.

Ravensbury Park

13 Continue along the Wandle Trail to Deen City Farm and cross over the small wooden bridge then the tram line level crossing (can be muddy here). Take care crossing (trams can be quiet and approach without warning). Follow the path and take the L-hand option where you see the signpost heading into Morden Hall Park, following NCN 20 signs to Morden Hall. Cross over the river using the small footbridges. Head L over the ornamental bridge then take the R-hand path and follow it to Morden Road.

14 At Morden Road turn R onto the pavement and use the toucan crossing. Turn R along the small residential road soon turning L into Ravensbury Park, following the path to keep the river on your R.

15 Turn right up the wooden walkway to the road, onto the shared use pavement along Bishopsford Road. Follow it for 200m. L at Bishopford Lodge (entry to Bishopford House).

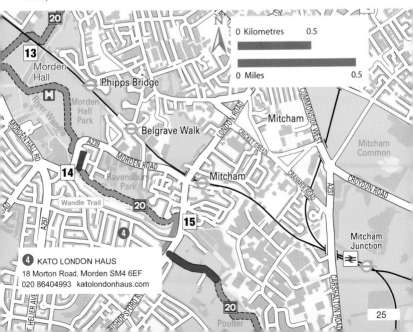

4 KATO LONDON HAUS
18 Morton Road, Morden SM4 6EF
020 86404993 katolondonhaus.com

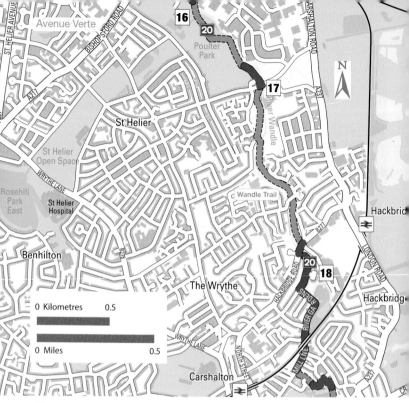

16 Split L off tarmac by the 5 aside football pitches onto crushed stone path. Descend to River Wandle and follow it on your L. Cross Middleton Road, bearing R then sharp L onto a riverside path.

17 Follow the river to cross it at the wooden bridge, continuing on to Culvers Avenue, which you cross to stay on the riverside path. When you reach Hackbridge Road, cross the road with care and continue westwards along it, before turning L onto the shared space and into The Causeway.

18 Head along The Causeway then turn L into River Gardens, which turns into Mill Lane. After the junction with Butter Hill, turn L into the segregated cycle path that runs along the river.

19 Soon turn L onto the bridge, and continue on the path until Arcadia Close. Follow the road to the left, turn right onto Parkfield Close then head straight onto the path that runs around the edge of the sports centre. At the end of the path turn L onto Westcroft Road towards the High Street (Carshalton).

20 At the High Street turn L, then turn immediately R onto Park Lane. Head up the hill as the road turns into Boundary Road, at the end of which you will see a country track that you should head L onto.

Avenue Verte above Carshalton

1 GREYHOUND HOTEL
High Street, Carshalton SM5 3PE
020 86471511 thegreyhoundhotel.com

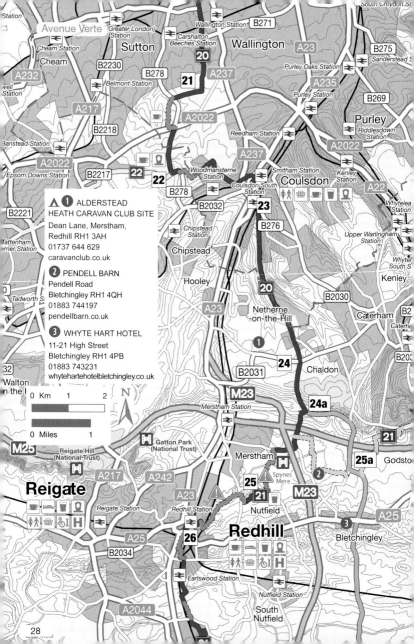

① ALDERSTEAD HEATH CARAVAN CLUB SITE
Dean Lane, Merstham,
Redhill RH1 3AH
01737 644 629
caravanclub.co.uk

② PENDELL BARN
Pendell Road
Bletchingley RH1 4QH
01883 744197
pendellbarn.co.uk

③ WHYTE HART HOTEL
11-21 High Street
Bletchingley RH1 4PB
01883 743231
whytehartehotelbletchingley.co.uk

0 Km   1   2

0 Miles   1

21 The narrow track leads to a conrete road where you turn R at a crossroads. Enjoy fantastic views as you descend. At the bottom turn R onto Woodmansterne Road, and then take a L when you see the Oaks Park sign, into the car park. Head through the park, passing the cafe. Head straight on through the wood with the path bearing L before you turn R, leaving the park over the toucan crossing. On the other side, head left onto the cycle track and follow it down until you reach Carshalton Road, turning R onto it.

22 At the junction turn L onto Rectory Lane, and head downhill before turning L at the sign for Hatch Lane (a narrow country path) on the L hand side. Carry on up the steep hill on the bumpy track. It eventually joins The Mount, a residential road. At the junction with The Grove turn R and descend steeply to a T-junction and L.
Straight on at Woodcote Grove Road onto The Avenue. Head downhill and turn R onto Brighton Road. Keep bearing L, before heading onto the shared use pavement just before the roundabout.

23 Follow this path around, crossing the arm of the roundabout using the toucan crossing, and rejoin the road as you head up the hill of Marlpit Lane (busy, take care). Soon take the second road on the R (Downs Road) then fork L onto Ditches Lane. Follow this quiet road through Farthing Down, which on a clear day has beautiful views of London and Surrey. Past a church fork R onto Church Lane.

24 Continue along Church Lane to cross over the main road in Chaldon onto Hilltop Lane as it runs steeply downhill. (See **24a** below for the quiet road alternative to Crawley Down). This road eventually turns into Warwick Wold Road that runs over the M25. Turn R onto Bletchingley Road and continue under the M23. After 400 metres turn L onto a path leading to a metal gate on your L. Head down this path through the nature reserve until it eventually meets Nutfield Marsh Road. Turn L and immediately R past the attractive Inn on the Pond. Just by the pub head R onto the track by the pond.

25 Continue past the cricket ground into Chilmead Lane to Cormongers Lane. Turn R onto a narrow path behind the hedge. Very soon turn L onto a traffic-free path through The Moors **(easy to miss)**, the last open countryside before Redhill. After following a stream on your L, split L by a pond.
The path emerges at Cavendish Road, where you turn R. Continue downhill, over a footbridge across Redhill Brook, then L into Noke Drive.

26 At the traffic lights turn R under the railway bridges and past the train station, with services to London, Gatwick and Brighton. Turn L at the roundabout into Marketfield Way (cycle lanes). At another railway bridge join the shared footway beside the A23 Brighton Road. Turn L into Brook Road, still on the shared footway. At the T-junction turn L to pass under the railway line again. Leave the footway and turn R into Earlsbrook Road.

Chaldon - Crawley Down alternative

This unsigned option uses mainly quiet roads to avoid the complex navigation through Redhill, Crawley and Gatwick. **However, note there are occasional sections on busier roads (especially at rush hour), so it is not advised for younger or very inexperienced riders.**

24a On the descent of Hilltop Lane L onto Spring Bottom Lane. R at T-junction onto Whitehill La, for Nutfield and Bletchingley.

25a L onto Place Farm Road, joining NCN21 briefly, before bending R onto tiny Church Lane. Enter lovely Bletchingley and carefully head straight over the A25 onto Outwood Lane.

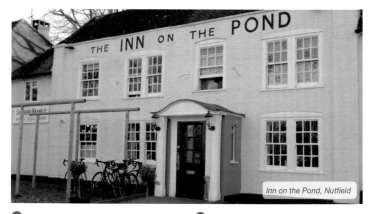

Inn on the Pond, Nutfield

1 BROMPTON GUEST HOUSE
6, Crossland Road, Redhill RH1 4AN
01737 765613 www.bromptonguesthouse.com

2 PREMIER INN REDHILL
Brighton Road,
Salfords, Redhill RH1 5BT
0871 527 8930 www.premierinn.com

3 CAMBRIDGE HOTEL GATWICK
19, Bonehurst Road, Horley RH6 8PP
01293 783990
www.gatwickcambridgehotel.co.uk

4 THE AMBERS GUEST HOUSE
7, Vicarage Lane, Horley RH6 8AR
01293 785649 www.theambersgatwick.com

5 SOUTHBOURNE GUEST HOUSE
34, Massetts Road, Horley RH6 7DS
01293 771991 www.southbournegatwick.com

6 THE LAWN GUEST HOUSE
30, Massetts Road, Horley RH6 7DF
01293 775751 www.lawnguesthouse.co.uk

7 THREE ACRES GUESTHOUSE
Reigate Road, Hookwood, Horley RH6 0AP
01293 426262 threeacresgatwick.co.uk

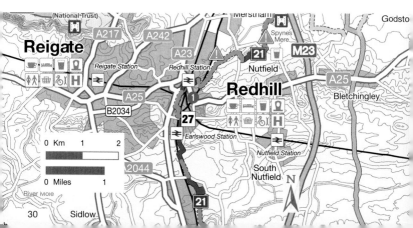

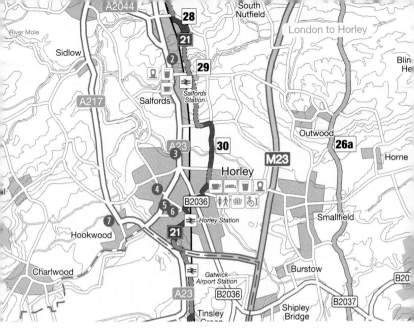

27 Continue straight ahead at the junction into Prince's Road (**easy to miss**), then R into Asylum Arch Road. Just before the arch under the railway, turn left onto an attractive tarmac path through woodland, parallel to the railway. Passing the modern East Surrey Hospital to the L, cross the busy road at the signal crossing and continue onto an unmade track.

28 Join Bushfield Drive, following roads through White Bushes housing area, bending L then turning R and R again. At the local shops turn L into Green Lane (a byway), into open countryside, leaving Redhill behind. After a short section between hedges, this becomes a concrete farm road through open fields.

29 Cross Honeycrock Lane, past a business park into another byway, which continues gently downhill through pleasant woodland. Emerge at the road and L then L again onto Cross Oak Lane. Shortly turn R into unmade Lake Lane.

30 Follow Lake Lane into Horley, joining Langshott Lane. Bear R, keeping on Langshott Lane which becomes cycleway then lane again, to a T-junction with Smallfield Road. R here and at the main road cross into Station Road. Look out for the the subway under the railway line (**easy to miss**), where you will need to dismount at busy times. The subway leads directly into the High Street, ideal for a well-earned rest at one of the local cafes.

Chaldon - Crawley Down alternative cont.

26a Having followed Outwood Lane for around 3.5 miles enter Outwood by the Bell Inn and the lovely common area with windmill. Just carry on, on Scott's Hill out of Outwood for just over 0.5 miles and then turn L onto the tiny Cogmans Lane. At the crossroads in Smallfield go straight over onto Dowlands Lane. Follow past Cross Lane to the B2037. Alternative route concludes on page 37.

The Forest Way runs between
East Grinstead and Groombridge

Horley ~ Groombridge

The phrase 'astounding contrasts' may be a guidebook cliche, but it really is the case here, as the route out of Horley brushes up against the main Gatwick runway, landing lights at the side of the tarmac cycle path, planes passing incredibly close overhead. After more modernity through Crawley you are soon in a timeless landscape, along the Worth Way, a wonderfully rural path along an old railway trackbed. After a brief urban interlude at East Grinstead there's more fine traffic-free riding along the Forest Way, dotted with prosperous, handsome villages such as Forest Row, Hartfield, Withyham and Groombridge, with their distinctive red tiled, half-timbered and lap-boarded architecture and ancient inns. The lovely country town of Royal Tunbridge Wells is a tempting 14.5 km (9 mile) there and back excursion from the main route.

Route Info

Distance 39 kilometres / 24 miles
Note Chaldon / Crawley Down shortcut is overall 8 miles shorter (pages 28-31 & 37)

Terrain & Route Surface The majority of this section is on the Worth and Forest Ways, unsurfaced traffic-free paths where mudguards are advisable, especially in the wet. Before this the going is mainly on tarmac, either minor urban roads or some surprisingly leafy and green cycle paths around Gatwick and Crawley. Although you climb gradually to East Grinstead the route evens out any sharp gradients and you are then able to coast down most of the way to Groombridge.

Off-road 43% traffic-free, mainly on the crushed stone, unsealed surface of the Worth and Forest Ways.

Profile

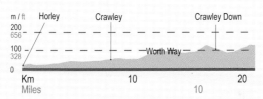

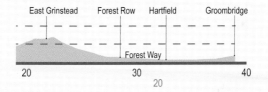

Hartfield village on the Forest Way

© Andrew Wilkinson Creative Commons

What to See & Do

• Gatwick Airport may not be classed as a tourist attraction by many, but the route past here is certainly spectacular and there is a lift from the cycle path used by the Avenue Verte directly to the airport terminal.

• **Tilgate Park** lies just southwest of the route as it leaves Crawley. It's easily accessible via the traffic-free section of NCN 20 here and has a nature centre (including Meerkats!), a walled garden and cafe amongst much else.

• The historic local market town of **East Grinstead** has a lovely wide high street with half-timbered buildings. East Grinstead Museum is a small local history museum with free admission.

The town is particularly proud of the lovely Sackville College Almshouses and the National Trust property of Standen, which is famous for its Arts and Crafts associations.

• The steam powered **Bluebell Railway** has its northern terminus at East Grinstead, with a recently built station there, allowing access to the main rail network. The southern terminus of Sheffield Park has a huge collection of old locomotives. www.bluebell-railway.com

• At **Forest Row** you'll find a picturesque town in a lovely setting on a hill above the River Medway.

• **Hartfield** is an old village which was a centre for iron production in the nineteenth century and later the setting for Winnie The Pooh.

• Whilst **Groombridge** is an attractive village in its own right, its old centre clustered around a lovely green, it is for the **Spa Valley Steam Railway** that the village is best known. With small stations at Eridge and Groombridge, this extremely popular tourist railway crosses picturesque, traditional Kent and Sussex landscapes for nearly 8 km (5 miles) to end at Royal Tunbridge Wells West station. The train runs on weekends and holidays from April to October. As the railway allows bicycles on board a good option, if you wish to follow National Cycle Network route 18 linking Royal Tunbridge Wells to Groombridge, might be to cycle in one direction and take the steam railway in another. www.spavalleyrailway.co.uk

Along the Worth Way

Directions

1 From pedestrianised Horley High Street turn L onto busy Victoria Road. Where the main road rises to cross the railway, turn R then immediately L into The Drive. Turn R onto Cheyne Walk and continue to a large roundabout and take the first exit. Turn R, L and R again and at last reach the Riverside Garden Park, an attractive green space on the edge of Horley. The route closely follows the Gatwick Stream on a traffic-free path through the heart of Gatwick Airport.

Through the park pass under the A23 (long subway) emerging alongside the elevated shuttle train that links the North and South airport terminals. Pass under the shuttle building and follow the road directly alongside the railway platform. As you pass under the station and airport buildings, keep an eye out for the lift up to the terminal and the station if you need the facilities here. The path rejoins the Gatwick Stream, passing under the flight path. Ironically this is one of the greenest sections of the route.

2 You soon come back to modern life at City Place commercial development. Join the shared footway on the L-hand side of Beehive Ring Road and continue on shared paths into Crawley, with signal crossings of Radford Road and Gatwick Road.

At a roundabout follow the footway R into Fleming Way, continue to the signal crossing and turn L into Newton Road. At the next major road turn R onto the footway and use the signal crossing to join the shared path. Join Woolborough Lane and pass under a major road (subway). Pick up the shared footway again; keep L then cross the road into an open space. Bear L and cross the road at a signal crossing. Turn L and immediately R to the junction of Routes 21 and 20 on North Road.

3 Route 21 continues ahead towards Three Bridges on Pond Wood Road, but the Avenue Verte follows Route 20 to the R on North Road. Bear L at the road junction and continue on North Road until it meets a T-junction. Turn L then R and bear R, past playing fields. At the football ground turn L then R beside a major road. Continue beside the road for Crawley town centre and railway station. Cross the road at the signals to join Tilgate Drive cycle track, a green lane lined with trees and hedges.

4 Continue on this track, crossing a road onto Furnace Farm Road to meet St Leonards Drive and turn L. Soon Route 20 bends R into Rosamund Road, but we continue ahead on a tree-lined path, under the railway line to emerge next to Oriel School. Skirt the school and use the signal to cross into Maidenbower Drive. Very soon head L over the road to join an attractive bridleway through woodland, eventually crossing the Gatwick Stream on a wooden footbridge. Turn R and immediately L, onto a path which climbs gently uphill to meet the old railway line, the Worth Way.

5 Pass under the Worth Way and turn right, climbing steeply to join the old railway. This is the start of a long section on former railways, a hugely attractive and largely traffic-free route all the way to the south coast. Pass under a subway, climb out of the railway cutting then turn R onto Church Road.

6 Turn L and just before the church bear L onto a wooded lane, which descends at first then climbs onto a substantial bridge over the M23. Leaving Crawley behind, enter open countryside on a wooded bridleway. At the next road turn L on a shared footway, then cross the road with care to rejoin the old railway towards Crawley Down.

7 Continue on the Worth Way until it emerges into Old Station Close (plenty of eating options at the end of here). Follow residential roads through Crawley Down to rejoin the railway path by a pond.

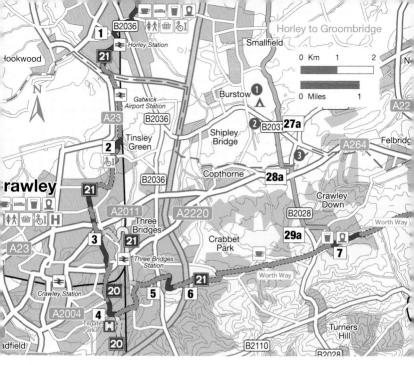

Accommodation

Chaldon - Crawley Down alternative continued from page 31

27a Meeting the B2037 at the end of Dowlands Lane turn R, with care, then very shortly L
onto Effingham Lane. Follow to bend L onto Mill Lane.

28a Meet the B2028 and R with care. Cross the main A264 roundabout with care.

29a 0.75 miles after the roundabout L onto Sandy Lane in Crawley Down. R onto Vicarage
Road and second L onto Station Road. At shops turn L onto Burleigh Way to rejoin official
Avenue Verte Route.

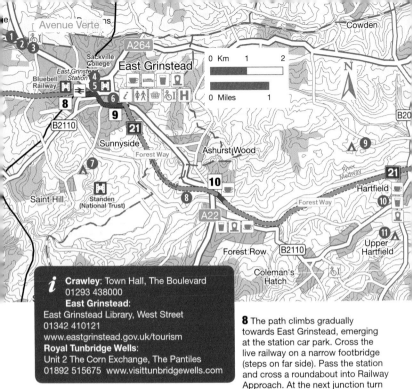

8 The path climbs gradually towards East Grinstead, emerging at the station car park. Cross the live railway on a narrow footbridge (steps on far side). Pass the station and cross a roundabout into Railway Approach. At the next junction turn R into the town centre (London Rd) with numerous shops and cafes. Over a crossroads then turn L into High Street with its attractive half-timbered buildings. Continue over a small roundabout onto the Lewes Road (B2110).

9 Just before the A22 turn R using a small section of cycleway at another roundabout to join the Forest Way to Groombridge. The Forest Way is another former railway, passing through the lovely High Weald with extensive views of rolling countryside. The path drops steeply to join the old railway alignment, crosses a road then passes through open countryside to Forest Row.

10 Forest Row village centre is worth the short detour off the Forest Way, with several interesting shops. Cross the A22 at the signal crossing and join the lane opposite (village R here along the busy A22). **Easy to miss!** Split R off the tarmac lane (straight on leads to farm shop and cafe) onto a narrow earth track signed Forest Way Country Park, and continue down the upper River Medway valley past Hartfield and Withyham.

1 PREMIER INN
London Road, Felbridge,
East Grinstead RH19 2QR
0871 527 8348 www.premierinn.com

2 CROWNE PLAZA HOTEL
London Road,Felbridge
East Grinstead RH19 2BH
01342 337700 www.ihg.com

3 GRINSTEAD LODGE GUEST HOUSE
London Road, East Grinstead RH19 1QE
01342 317222 grinsteadlodge.co.uk

4 ST PETERS HOUSE
55 Moat Road, East Grinstead RH19 3LJ
01342 314624

5 CRANSTON HOUSE GUEST HOUSE
Cranston Road, East Grinstead RH19 3HW
01342 323609 www.cranstonhouse.co.uk
Secure cycle storage

6 GOTHIC HOUSE ACCOMMODATION
55, High Street, East Grinstead RH19 3DD
01342 301910 cjscafebar.com
On the route

▲ 7 EVERGREEN FARM CAMPSITE
West Hoathly Road, East Grinstead RH19 4NE
01342 327720

8 BRAMBLETYE MANOR BARN
Brambletye Lane, Forest Row RH18 5EH
01342 826866 www.brambletyemanorbarn.co.uk

▲ 9 ST IVES FARM
Butcherfield Lane, Hartfield TN7 4JX
01892 770213 www.stivesfarm.co.uk
Around 1 km (0.6 miles) from the route

10 THE ANCHOR
Church Street, Hartfield TN7 4AG
01892 770424
anchorhartfield.com

▲ 11 HARTFIELD – STAIRS FARM
Jib Jacks Hill, Hartfield TN7 4DQ
07526618841
Around 1 km (0.6 miles) from the route

There are rail stations at Gatwick Airport (served by Great Western Railway, Southern, Thameslink and the Gatwick Express), Crawley-Three Bridges (Southern and Thameslink) and East Grinstead (Southern). These are all close to the Avenue Verte.
Groombridge has no station itself but there is one at Ashurst (Southern) about 4 km (2.5 miles) to the north. Eridge, 4 km (2.5 miles) along the Avenue Verte to the south of Groombridge, has a station (Southern) which is also the terminus for the Spa Valley Railway heritage line, which runs up to Royal Tunbridge Wells and carries bikes.
Royal Tunbridge Wells main line station (Southeastern) is around 0.8 km (0.5 miles) from the Spa Valley Railway terminus.
Bikes on trains policies:
Great Western Railway
Reservation advised where possible 0345 700 0125 www.gwr.com
Southeastern
Peak hour restrictions on services to and from London, although no restrictions going south from Tonbridge 0345 322 7021 www.southeasternrailway.co.uk

Royal Tunbridge Wells
© Creative Commons grassrootsgroundswell

11 At the old railway junction in Groombridge the path runs through fields alongside the live railway, emerging onto a lane to the south of the village.
The village centre is up to the L whilst the main route continues on minor roads to the R. Groombridge has a couple of shops and a pub but the main attraction is the Spa Valley Railway, which runs to Tunbridge Wells.
The cycle ride on Route 18 is also attractive, passing woodland and the rock formations at High Rock **12**
A good option is to take the steam train in one direction and cycle the other way.
Tunbridge Wells is a large town with good facilities and the famous Georgian colonnaded walkway known as The Pantiles.

1 THE CROWN INN
Groombridge TN3 9QH
01892 864742 www.thecrowngroombridge.com
Around 1 km (0.6 miles) from the route

▲ 2 MANOR COURT FARM
Ashurst, Tunbridge Wells TN3 9TB
01892 740210 www.manorcourtfarm.co.uk
Campsite and bed and breakfast about 2 km
(1.25 miles) from route

3 THE RUSSELL HOTEL
80, London Road,
Royal Tunbridge Wells TN1 1DZ
01892 544833 www.russell-hotel.com

4 THE BRICK HOUSE B & B
21 Mount Ephraim Road,
Royal Tunbridge Wells TN1 1EN
01892 516517 www.thebrickhousebandb.co.uk

5 THE VICTORIAN BED & BREAKFAST
22 Lansdowne Road
Royal Tunbridge Wells TN1 2NJ
01892 533633 www.thevictorianbandb.com

There is also a Travelodge at Mount Ephraim,
Tunbridge Wells, TN4 8BU 0871 984 6381. It is
on the A264 to the west of the town centre.

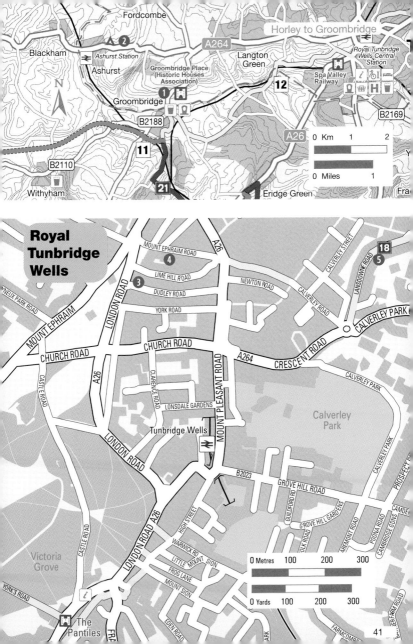

Fordcombe

Horley to Groombridge

Blackham

A264

Langton
Green

Royal Tunbridge
Wells Central
Station

Ashurst Station

2

Ashurst

Groombridge Place
(Historic Houses
Association)

Spa Valley
Railway

12

1

Groombridge

B2169

B2188

11

A26

0 Km 1 2

B2110

0 Miles 1

Withyham

21

Eridge Green

Fra

Royal
Tunbridge
Wells

MOUNT EPHRAIM ROAD

A26

CALVERLEY STREET

LANSDOWNE ROAD

18

4

5

'NFLUX PARK ROAD

LONDON ROAD

LIME HILL ROAD

3

NEWTON ROAD

CALVERLEY ROAD

DUDLEY ROAD

MOUNT EPHRAIM

YORK ROAD

CALVERLEY PARK

CHURCH ROAD

CHURCH ROAD

A26

CRESCENT ROAD

CASTLE ROAD

CLARENCE ROAD

CALVERLEY PARK

LONSDALE GARDENS

MOUNT PLEASANT ROAD

Calverley
Park

Tunbridge Wells

LONDON ROAD

B2023

GROVE HILL ROAD

PROSPECT

HIGH STREET

GUILDFORD RD

GROVE HILL GARDENS

FOLK ROAD

CLAREMONT ROAD

PODNA ROAD

CAMBRIDGE EDNS

CAMDE

Victoria
Grove

CASTLE ROAD

LONDON ROAD A26

WARWICK RD

LITTLE MOUNT SION

0 Metres 100 200 300

FROG LANE

MOUNT SION

0 Yards 100 200 300

YORK'S ROAD

The
Pantiles

FR

ARK

EDEN RD

FARMCOMP

41

The Avenue Verte passes close
to the south coast by Seven
Sisters Country Park

Groombridge ~ Newhaven

The fine villages of Rotherfield and Mayfield are found along the route, as you dip and climb on a minor road across the High Weald. Weald is the old English word for forest and this area still retains around a quarter of its original thick blanket of trees. At Heathfield you start a gentle 122 metre (400 feet) drop along the wide, excellently-surfaced tarmac of the Cuckoo Trail to Polegate. As well as being a former railway, the Cuckoo Trail is something of a haven for wildlife, including cuckoos. Your final descent, to the English Channel and the ferry that awaits you at Newhaven, takes you through a picturesque gap in the South Downs, the Cuckmere Valley and the south coast's famed chalk white cliffs at the Seven Sisters Country Park.

Route Info

Distance 67 kilometres / 42 miles

Terrain & Route Surface Whilst this is a relatively long section it's downhill towards the coast, especially once you have crossed the ups and downs of the High Weald at the start. If you are taking it very easy and want to break overnight halfway then Heathfield is a very handy place to do so.
From Heathfield the going really couldn't be easier, as you follow the well- surfaced Cuckoo Trail, cross the Cuckmere Valley on quiet roads and finish on a traffic-free run along the coast into Newhaven. Off-road sections are mostly tarmac.

Off-road 43% mainly good quality tarmac. One short unsealed woodland track west of Polegate at the end of the Cuckoo Trail.

Profile

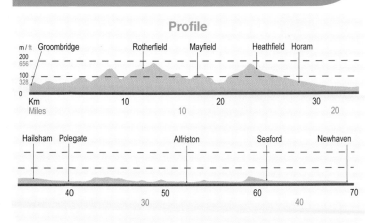

43

What to See & Do

• **The High Weald's rolling farmland and forests** provide some testing cycling, with short but stiff climbs. The reward is a succession of lovely country viewpoints and villages. **Mayfield** High Street, just off the route, is a wonderful opportunity to break in attractive surroundings. www.highweald.org

• It's particularly apt that **Heathfield** hosts an **Anglo-French market** every August Bank Holiday Monday. Just south of Heathfield on the Cuckoo Trail at **Horam** is the Sussex Farm Museum.

• **Knockhatch Adventure Park,** near Hailsham, boasts birds of prey, crazy golf, mini-quad and bungee trampolines amongst the many attractions of its 80 acres.

• **Michelham Priory**, some 4 km (2.5miles) west of the Cuckoo Trail at Hailsham is an impressive Augustinian priory with a watermill powered by the surrounding moat.

• The **Low Weald** is only around 8 km (5 miles) wide, extending from Polegate east to Ditchling and Hellingly. This broad, low-lying, gently undulating clay vale underlies a small scale intimate landscape with an intricate mix of copses and shaws, a patchwork of fields and hedgerows.

• **Drusillas Zoo** is a blend of action packed activities and a serious, conservation-minded zoo. They hold the studbook for rockhopper penguins and capybara (studbooks being important conservation documents).

Alfriston's lovely main street

Meet the coast at Seaford

• The **Long Man of Wilmington hill** figure can just be glimpsed from the route on the section near Drusillas Zoo. It is 69.2 metres (227 ft) tall, holds two "staves", and though formerly thought to originate in the Iron Age archaeological work has shown that it may have been cut in the 16th or 17th century AD.

• **Alfriston** is a beautifully preserved South Downs village, sheltering in the Cuckmere Gap. The **National Trust's Clergy House** is a medieval thatched cottage and was the first property they acquired back in 1896. The beautiful 14th century church, surrounded by the peaceful and expansive Tye (village green), and a 15th century inn are also amongst Alfriston's fine collection of old buildings.

• Just south of Litlington a lovely view opens up across the Cuckmere Valley to National Trust owned Cradle Hill. Look out for the **white horse** cut into the chalk on the steep scarp there. It dates from 1836.

Also in the area is High and Over's dramatic river cliff which has been carved out of the soft chalk by the river below.

• The **South Downs National Park** was only granted its status in 2011 and is the UK's newest National Park. Known for stunning views from chalk ridges and cliffs it also includes the contrasting wooded countryside of the High Weald (see above) www.southdowns.gov.uk

• Situated just off the route as you approach the south coast, the **Seven Sisters Country Park** can certainly claim to have a landscape synonymous with Britishness; the sisters in question are towering chalk cliffs typical of the area. www.sevensisters.org.uk

• If you fancy continuing cycling west from Newhaven for nearly 16 km (10 miles) **NCN route 2** will bring you to **Brighton**. It is most famous for the Royal Pavilion, an extravagant Eastern-inspired construction and former palace. Also look out for The Lanes, a maze of shops, cafes and bars. NCN 2 is a fantastic ride, passing under white cliffs and entering Brighton alongside its expansive beach. Another option for seeing its attractions is to catch the train from Polegate and cycle back to Newhaven.

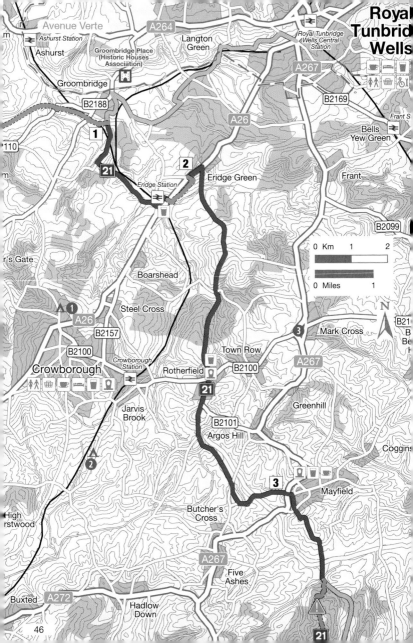

Directions

The next few miles between Groombridge and Heathfield cross the High Weald on quiet lanes, passing small woodlands and hilltop villages. There are no big hills, but several short steep climbs, meaning that this is the most physically demanding section of the route between London and Newhaven.

1 At the end of the Forest Way turn R then at the next junction turn L into Forge Road. Turn L, to pass Eridge station, then R through a wooden gate, passing The Lodge on your L, and under the A26. Turn L and climb up a rough bridleway which runs alongside the main road.

2 The bridleway joins a length of old road, briefly coming alongside the A26. The roadside cycleway bears R onto a minor road to descend, at the end of which turn R. The road undulates through woodland and pasture before climbing to the attractive village of Rotherfield with a few shops and a couple of pubs. At the T-junction here head L onto the high street.

Continue through Rotherfield on the B2101 and where the 2101 turns L, go straight on, onto quiet country lanes. At a fork in the road turn L, signed Five Ashes and Heathfield, and drop steeply. Just starting to climb turn L onto Fir Toll Road. Bear L at the next junction,

3 Outside Mayfield village carefully cross the A267 and climb steeply the other side to emerge close to the site of the old station. The route turns R, away from the village, but we recommend a short diversion along Station Road into the High Street, which has several shops and pubs. Shortly turn L and bend R to climb Knowle Hill which becomes Newick Lane.

Accommodation

⚠ ❶ CROWBOROUGH CAMPING AND CARAVANNING CLUB SITE
Goldsmith Recreation Ground, Eridge Road
Crowborough TN6 2TN   01892 664827
www.campingandcaravanningclub.co.uk
90 pitch club site – non-members welcome
About 4 km (2.5 miles) from the route

⚠ ❷ IDLE HOURS CAMPSITE
Owlsbury Park, Hadlow Down Road
Crowborough TN6 3SA
07787 945667

❸ ROSE COTTAGE
Mill Ln, Mark Cross TN6 3PJ
01892 852592
rosecottagemarkcross.co.uk

There are no train stations on the route south of Eridge until you reach Polegate (Southern - see page 21 for bike carrying policy). Stations at Berwick and Southease are near the Avenue Verte. Seaford and Newhaven stations are on the route and are on a branch line. Newhaven has a town station and a harbour station, the town station being the one to use for the ferry port as it is pretty much adjacent to the ferry terminal.

Travel from London involves a change at Lewes (around 1 hour 20 mins from London Victoria), although you can travel direct to Brighton from London Victoria and London Bridge then ride the lovely NCN 2 to Newhaven which is around 16 km (10 miles).

The ferry service for Dieppe has a morning sailing and late night sailing and takes around four hours. Times vary according to the tide. Possible evening sailing in summer.

www.transmanche.co.uk See page 12 for more information on travelling by ferry.

4 At Old Mill Farm there is a choice of route. Route 21 turns right and follows a bridleway across a field and climbs up through woodland. The surface improves on higher ground, but can be muddy and difficult after rainfall. The alternative route is to continue on Newick Lane, which climbs steadily up to the A265 main road.

5 Route 21 on Marklye Lane (the off-road option) emerges at A265 traffic lights, crossing straight over into Tower Street. The alternative route joins the A265 for a short distance, turning L into Tower Street.

R off Tower St and follow well-signed residential roads to the start of the Cuckoo Trail off Station Road (handy Waitrose and cafe nearby). The centre of Heathfield is a short distance up the hill, with a full range of shops and services spread along the High Street. A short diversion to the old Heathfield Tunnel is worth the effort as it was restored and reopened to the public a few years ago. The tunnel runs under the High Street and leads to an attractive open space, a pleasant spot for a picnic.

1 IWOOD BED AND BREAKFAST
Mutton Hall Lane, Heathfield TN21 8NR
01435 863918 www.iwoodbb.com
Secure storage for bicycles

2 THIMBLES
New Pond Hill, Cross in Hand, Heathfield, East Sussex TN21 0NB
01435 860745 thimblesbedandbreakfast.co.uk

3 RUNT IN TUN
Camping and Caravanning Club Site
Maynards Green, Heathfield TN21 0DJ
01435 864284 www.runtintun.co.uk
By the route

▲ **4** HORAM MANOR TOURING PARK
Horam, Heathfield TN21 0YD
01435 813662 horam-manor.co.uk
About 1 km (0.6 miles) from the route

▲ **5** WOODLAND VIEW TOURING PARK
Horebeech Lane, Horam TN21 0HR
01435 813597
www.woodlandviewtouringpark.co.uk

6 WIMBLES
Foords Lane, Vines Cross TN21 9HA
01435 810390 experiencesussex.co.uk
Cyclists Welcome. 2 km (1.25 miles) from the route.

▲ **7** FONTMILLS FARM CAMPSITE
North Street, Hellingly BN27 4EB
01435 813930 fontmills.co.uk
Accessible from the route (Cuckoo Trail)

8 FONTMILLS HOUSE B&B
Address above 01435 812703 fontmillshouse.co.uk

9 TRAVELODGE
A22 Boship Farm Roundabout
Hellingly BN27 4DP
01435 810390 travelodge.co.uk

10 LONGLEYS FARM COTTAGE
Harebeating Lane, Hailsham BN27 1ER
01323 841227 longleysfarmcottage.co.uk

Rotherfield's lovely architecture

1 THE HOMESTEAD
Ersham Road, Hailsham BN27 3PN
01323 840346 Possibly CCC members only
www.campingandcaravanningclub.co.uk
About 1 km (0.6 miles) from the route

2 PEEL HOUSE FARM CARAVAN PARK
Sayerland Lane, Polegate BN26 6QX
01323 845629 www.peelhousefarm.com

3 CUCKOOS REST CAMPING
Peel Cottage, Sayerlands Lane,
Polegate BN26 6QX
07564 518 576 cuckoosrest.webedn.co.uk

4 PREMIER INN
Hailsham Road, Polegate, Eastbourne BN26 6QL
0871 527 8354 premierinn.com

5 ALFRISTON CAMPING PARK
Pleasant Rise Farm, Alfriston BN26 5TN
alfristoncamping.co.uk Open all year About 1.5
km (1 mile) from the route

6 BARN OWLS SELF CATERING COTTAGES
Foxhole Farm, Seaford Road, Newhaven BN9 0EE
01273 513760 barn-owls.moonfruit.co.uk
Self catering and bed and breakfast about 1 km
(0.6 miles) from Newhaven, by the route

ALFRISTON ACCOMMODATION
Alfriston options include Chestnuts
Tearoom B & B 01323 870959, George Inn
01323 870319, Highcroft 01323 870553,
Riverdale 01323 871038, Star Inn 01323 870495,
Wingrove House 01323 870276, Deans Place
Hotel 01323 870248.

SEAFORD ACCOMMODATION
Options include Malvern House 01323 492058,
The Avondale 01323 890008, Brecon Guest
Accommodation 01323 892911, Cranleigh House
01323 893113, Florence House 01323 873700,
Hill House 01323 899759, Holmes Lodge 01323
898331, The White Lion Hotel 01323 892473 and
The Wellington Hotel 01323 899517. Saltmarsh
Farmhouse 01323 870218 is at Seven Sisters
Country Park between Alfriston and Seaford.

AB FAB ROOMS BED AND BREAKFAST
11, Station Road, Bishopstone BN25 2RB
01323 895001 abfabrooms.co.uk
Just off the route 3.5 km (2 miles) from Newhaven

The mostly tarmac Cuckoo Trail runs gently downhill to Polegate, passing through a number of towns and villages with several pubs and cafes. **6** There are two short on-road sections in Hailsham. Firstly, briefly follow the Cedars. Secondly, just under South Road Bridge head L across the car park then R onto Station Rd. Just after the pond on the L, turn R into Lindfield Drive, and immediate L to join the trail.

7 Just before the footbridge over the A27, turn right onto a path by the main road, signed Abbots Wood. Continue beside a minor road, under the A22, and follow round to the R. Turn L onto a tree-lined bridleway (can be muddy in places after rain). Bear L by Cophall Farm and L at the next split. At a crossing of tracks bear L to join a tarmac lane. Head R and R again, onto Bayleys La. Left at the next T-junction to pass Arlington tea-garden, following the road to the Yew Tree Inn in where you bend L.

8 At the crossroads with Berwick station to the R head onto Common Lane then almost straight away turn L onto the Berwick Way, a path beside the road. At the end of the path join the road and continue to the roundabout on the A27. Use the signal crossing to join Alfriston Road past Drusillas Zoo Park.

9 The official route bypasses Alfriston but it is well worth a visit (the quietest approach, though hilly, is down Winton Street and West Street, rejoining the Avenue Verte using the off-road South Downs Way, crossing the river Cuckmere with magnificent views of the village) . Back on the route turn R in Lullington and follow the valley down towards the coast, passing through tiny Litlington on the way.

10 At the A259 turn R onto the main road (narrow footway for those nervous of heavy traffic). The road option continues up the main road to the edge of Seaford where it turns L, but there is an alternative unsurfaced route across the fields. Cross the river at Exceat Bridge, then turn L at the Golden Galleon and join a rough track beside the river (can be muddy after rain). Pass through a gate and turn R uphill over grass pasture.

11 At the edge of Seaford, turn L into Chyngton Lane to rejoin the official route. Turn R onto Chyngton Way. At the corner of the golf course turn left up Southdown Road, then R into Corsica Road, which leads at last to the seafront with views over the Channel. Turn R and follow the Esplanade through Seaford. Join the seafront cycle track by the Martello Tower.

12 Continue through Bishopstone and onto the excellent shared path beside the A259, with views over the Nature Reserve. Follow the path into Newhaven past retail parks and on to the entrance to the ferry port.

1 PREMIER INN
Avis Road, Newhaven BN9 0AG
0871 527 8810 www.premierinn.com

2 NEWHAVEN LODGE GUEST HOUSE
12, Brighton Road, Newhaven BN9 9NB
01273 513736 www.newhavenlodge.co.uk

YOUTH HOSTELS
There are YHA Hostels within about 5 km (3 miles) and 8 km (5 miles) of Newhaven. YHA South Downs at Beddingham BN8 6JS (0345 371 9574) halfway between Newhaven and Lewes, is open all year and is a 5 minute train ride north of Newhaven (Southease station).

BRIGHTON ACCOMMODATION
16 km (10 miles) from Newhaven, Brighton has a range of accommodation on offer. The centrally placed Kipps Hostel (01273 604182) offers both dormitory and private room accommodation and is one of a number of hostels in the town. There are chain hotels such as the Premier Inn (0871 527 8150), private ones small and large and many bed and breakfast guesthouses.

Alfriston, seen from the Avenue Verte

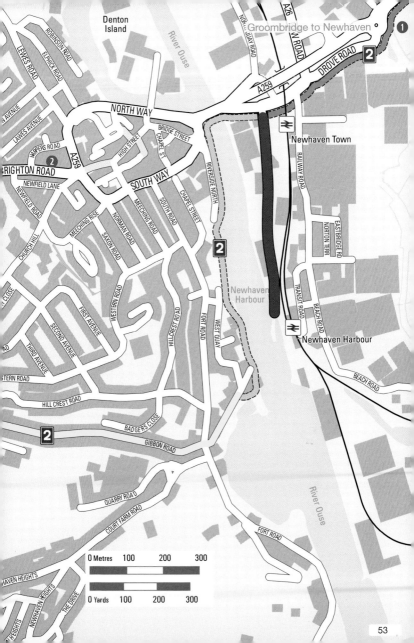

Denton
Island

River Ouse

2

1

A26

NORTH JUAN ROAD

DROVE ROAD

A259

Newhaven Town

ROBINSON ROAD

ELPHICK ROAD

LEWES ROAD

LAVES AVENUE

AVENUE

NORTH WAY

HIGH STREET

BRIDGE STREET

CHAPEL ST

NAPERS ROAD

A259

BRIGHTON ROAD

2

SOUTH WAY

RIVERSIDE NORTH

RAILWAY ROAD

NEWFIELD LANE

NEWFIELD ROAD

MEECHING RISE

NORMAN ROAD

MEECHING ROAD

SOUTH ROAD

CHAPEL STREET

EASTBRIDGE RD

NORTON TERR

CHURCH HILL

SAXON ROAD

WESTERN ROAD

HILLCREST ROAD

FORT ROAD

WEST QUAY

Newhaven
Harbour

2

TRANSIT ROAD

BEACH ROAD

CLOSE

FIRST AVENUE

SECOND AVENUE

THIRD AVENUE

STERN ROAD

RD

Newhaven Harbour

HILL CREST ROAD

BADGER'S CLOSE

GIBBON ROAD

2

BEACH ROAD

QUARRY ROAD

COURT FARM ROAD

FORT ROAD

River Ouse

HAVEN HEIGHTS

NEWHAVEN HEIGHTS

THE DRIVE

HEIGHTS

0 Metres   100   200   300

0 Yards   100   200   300

Dieppe's attractive harbour
welcomes you to France

Dieppe ~ Neufchâtel-en-Bray

Dieppe is a fine introduction to France; its lively harbour, packed in between dramatic cliffs, ensures a constant supply of fresh seafood to the restaurants that line it. Out of town you pass through attractive Arques-la-Bataille and its pretty, watery surroundings before joining one of the best cycle paths you'll find anywhere, the *Avenue Verte du Pays de Bray*, a wide, superbly surfaced path with nearby village services conveniently signed off the trail. There are long-term plans to extend the magnificent traffic-free section back into the heart of Dieppe. As well as the small-scale delights of village cafes and bars you should keep an eye out for the magnificent château at Mesnières.

Attractive Neufchâtel-en-Bray is a convenient and comfortable stopping off point, right by the trail and furnished with accommodation and plenty of bars and restaurants.

Route Info

Distance 37 kilometres / 23 miles

Terrain & Route Surface After negotiating the traffic of Dieppe's centre you are on the superb route along an old railway line that currently runs from Arques-la-Bataille to Forges-les-Eaux. The gradients are easy and there are plenty of charming villages right next to the route.

Off-road 77% traffic-free on wide, smooth tarmac.

Profile

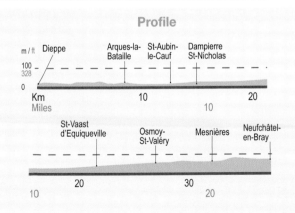

What to See & Do

• **Dieppe** has a reputation as one of the less industrial northern French ports and there's much to do and enjoy in this attractive small town. A climb to the small chapel of Notre-Dame-de-Bon-Secours lets you appreciate the dramatic setting of the harbour, packed between cliffs. The town museum in the Château de Dieppe just to the west of the front is also a great viewpoint. The lovely seafront lawns are a good place for a stroll, or those with younger cyclists might want to visit the aquariums of Cité de la Mer. Seafood dining is the main evening activity.• **Arques-la-Bataille**, currently the start of a superb section of traffic-free route, has a handy cluster of shops, cafes and restaurants at its heart and also preludes some fine riding through the lakes of the Varenne outdoor and watersports centre, overlooked by the crumbling remains of a medieval castle.

Sedate traffic-free riding at Neufchâtel-en-Bray

The château at Mesnières-en-Bray

• **Guy Weber Education Centre** at St-Aubin-le-Cauf is in a lovely riverside setting and home to various animals. Free entry. parcguyweber.free.fr

• It's hard to miss the **magnificent château** right by the route at **Mesnières-en-Bray**, around 6 km (4 miles) before the small, attractive town of Neufchâtel-en-Bray. Open to the public from Easter to 1st November.

57

Avenue Verte

Dieppe
pont Jehan Ango
02.32.14.40.60 dieppetourisme.com
Neufchâtel-en-Bray
6 place Notre-Dame 02.35.93.22.96
ot-pays-neufchatelois.fr

58

Dieppe

Hilly Scenic Route

3a Follow your nose and shortly after passing under the D485 bear R at a junction at the edge of the village (L goes to industrial units).

4a Coming into Martin Eglise head R at two T junctions then L onto D1 for Arques les Bataille. Follow the road into Arques-les-Batailles and R at a roundabout. Just over the level crossing pick up the traffic-free trail on the L by the Bar de la Gare.

1 LE MANOIR DE NEUVILLE-LÈS-DIEPPE
32 rue du Général de Gaulle
76370 Neuville-lès-Dieppe
02 35 83 99 53
manoirdeneuville.fr

2 GÎTE D'IMBLEVAL
chemin d'Imbleval
76370 Martin-Église
02 35 04 45 76
fdemonchy@wanadoo.fr

3 AUBERGE DU CLOS NORMAND
22, rue Henri IV - 76370 Martin-Eglise
02 35 40 40 40   closnormand.fr/en/

4 HÔTEL L'EOLIENNE
20, rue de la Croix de Pierre
76370 Rouxmesnil Bouteilles
02 32 14 40 00   hoteleolienne.com

△ 5 CAMPING VITAMIN
865, rue des Vertus 76550 Saint-Aubin-sur-Scie
02 35 82 11 11   www.camping-vitamin.com
Open March – October. About 1 km (0.6 miles)
from the route

6 B&B CLÉOME
23, rue de la Chaussée
76880 Arques-la-Bataille
02 35 84 16 56 www.cleomechambredhote.fr
On the route about 7 km (4.5 miles) from Dieppe

7 LA CHATELLENIE CHAMBRES D'HÔTES
268 route de la source
76510 Saint Aubin le Cauf
02 35 85 88 69
lachatellenie.com

△ 8 VARENNE PLEIN AIR
Base de loisirs, rue des Lannays
76510 St-Aubin-le-Cauf
02 35 85 69 05
varennepleinair.fr
Gîtes, rooms, dorms G

△ 9 CAMPING DES 2 RIVIÈRES
76880 Martigny
02 35 85 60 82
www.camping-2-rivieres.com

Dieppe - Paris (St-Lazare) trains take around 2 hours 15 mins, with a change necessary at Rouen. Only selected trains from Paris carry bikes but most services on the 45 min journey from Rouen do.
After Dieppe there are no stations on or near this section of route.
www.voyages-sncf.com

Continue for 24 km (15 miles) on the fantastic smooth tarmac surface all the way to Neufchâtel. You can do this very quickly, but we recommend that you take your time and visit some of the attractive villages along the route, most very close to the old railway, just a minute or two to bars, cafes and boulangeries.

7 One place worth a stop is the Guy Weber educational natural park just after the start of the railway path at St-Aubin-le-Cauf. This is free to enter and a great place for a picnic or a stroll beside the river Béthune .

Béthune valley scenery

▲ **❶** CAMPING DE L'ORIVAL
885 rue d'Orival,
76950 Les Grandes-Ventes
02 35 83 45 90 campinglorival.com

© Joël Damase

Forges-les-Eaux

• **Forges-les-Eaux** is a spa town with pretty villas dating from the Belle Époque period of history at the end of the 19th century. Further back in history Louis XIII, Anne of Austria and Cardinal Richelieu all came to take the waters here. A 19th century casino (sitting opposite the large attractive Epinay park and lake Andelle) added to the town's reputation as a high class resort. Good collection of local museums, including the museum of the French Resistance and another featuring models of horse-drawn vehicles. Small attractive town centre clustered around the distinctive town hall.

• **Gournay-en-Bray** is a market town that suffered much destruction in World War II but has been attractively restored. Excellent market in the town centre Tuesday and Friday mornings.

67

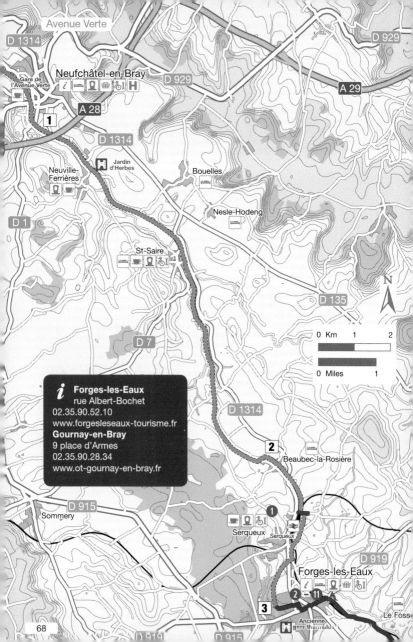

Avenue Verte

D 1314

D 929

Neufchâtel-en-Bray

D 929

A 29

A 28

1

D 1314

Neuville-Ferrières

Jardin d'Herbes

Bouelles

Nesle-Hodeng

D 1

St-Saire

N

D 135

D 7

0 Km 1 2

0 Miles 1

D 1314

i **Forges-les-Eaux**
rue Albert-Bochet
02.35.90.52.10
www.forgeleseaux-tourisme.fr
Gournay-en-Bray
9 place d'Armes
02.35.90.28.34
www.ot-gournay-en-bray.fr

2

Beaubec-la-Rosière

D 915

Sommery

1

Serqueux

Serqueux

D 919

Forges-les-Eaux

2 — 11

3

Ancienne

Le Foss

D 919

D 915

Directions

1 Continue on the traffic-free path away from Neufchâtel-en-Bray, climbing gradually up the Béthune Valley.

2 At Beaubec-la-Rosière, where the railway path comes to an end at the main line railway, the route continues on a traffic-free path, accessed by going L then immediate R under the live railway. Emerge at a road on Serqueux's outskirts. Turn R and prepare for the first hill after leaving Dieppe! Pass over the railway again then turn L onto another path. Bear R at the fork where this becomes a narrow lane and cross over a main road into a byway. This soon leads into a zigzag ramp onto another short section of railway path.

You have crossed the watershed between the Béthune and Epte valleys, so this section is delightfully downhill into Forges (take care not to miss the yellow diversion signs for the town centre on the left). It is possible to continue to the end of the line where you will see an old station building and on your right the monumental gate of Gisors.

3 Back to the diversion, follow the yellow signs through quiet residential streets. Turn R at a school to pass the imposing church down to rue de la République, where you turn L for the town centre.

Accommodation

If you want a longer first day on the French part of the route, Forges-les-Eaux is around 50 km (31 miles) from Dieppe

1 B&B LE COQ À L'ÂNE
1974 rue de la cote du bastringue,
76440 Beaubec La Rosière
02 35 09 17 91 lecoqalane.fr

2 L'HÔTEL LE CONTINENTAL
106 avenue des Sources
76440 Forges-les-Eaux
02 32 89 50 50 hotel-lecontinental.com

3 LES CHAMBRES DU LAC
34 bis rue d'Enghien, 76440 Forges-les-Eaux
06 52 25 36 02 leschambres-dulac.com

4 HÔTEL LA PAIX
15 rue de Neufchâtel 76440 Forges-les-Eaux
02 35 90 51 22 hotellapaix.fr

5 FORGES HOTEL
avenue des Sources 76440 Forges-les-Eaux
02 32 89 50 57 forgeshotel.com/en/

6 HÔTEL ST DENIS
1 rue de la libération 76440 Forges-les-Eaux
02 35 90 50 70 hotellesaintdenis.fr/en/

7 À LA MAISON DU LAC
28 avenue des Bouleaux
76440 Forges-les-Eaux
06 12 82 62 15 alamaisondulac.fr

8 HÔTEL SOFHOTEL
57 rue du Maréchal Leclerc
76440 Forges-les-Eaux
02 35 90 44 51
logishotels.com/en/hotel/hotel-sofhotel-150129

9 LE RELAIS DE LA CHASSE MARÉE
rue gare de Forges Thermal
76440 Forges-les-Eaux
02 35 09 68 37 www.lerelaisduchassemaree.fr
Group

10 LES HAUTS BRULINS
20 bis boulevard Nicolas Thiessé
76440 Forges-les-Eaux
02 35 90 83 34 http://les-hauts-brulins.com/
First floor flat with kitchen for up to three people

A **11** CAMPING LA MINIÈRE
3 boulevard Nicolas Thiesse
76440 Forges-les-Eaux
02 35 90 53 91 campingforges.com/en

The section from Forges to Gournay is very different to the railway path and younger children may find the ups and downs and twists and turns quite challenging. The route passes through an undulating landscape on minor roads. Although it does pass through a number of villages, there are very few facilities – the author did not see a single shop in 27 km (17 miles).

4 From the centre of Forges take the D915 for a short distance towards Gournay then turn L at Hôtel Le St Denis onto rue de la Republique (D919). Cross the old railway then immediately go R into a very quiet road passing fields and farmhouses. Continue beside the railway line until you come to a T-junction.

5 Turn R here, cross the railway then turn immediately L. This railway line is planned to form the extension of the railway path from Forges through to Gournay. At the next junction turn L onto the D61 and cross the railway again at La Bellière. Continue on the D61 through Pommereux, climbing steadily to a crossroads where you go straight ahead. At the next junction fork R for the D120 to Haussez (poor surface here, care required).

6 In Haussez turn R three times in succession to join the D41. Under the railway bridge go immediate L on a very quiet lane. Cross the river Epte then climb steadily out of the valley to Ménerval, a small village with a huge church. Just before you reach the watertower bear L. This is one of the highest points on the route between Forges and Gournay and you can look forward to several kilometres downhill.

7 Keep an eye out for the Avenue Verte sign as there is a sharp R then L that is easy to miss as you pick up speed down the D16 towards Dampierre-en-Bray. If you do miss this turn you will pick up the route again after the loop through Dampierre. In Dampierre turn R then L onto the D84.

8 Turn right at the roundabout onto the D16 for Gournay, then turn left after a short distance to Cuy-St-Fiacre.

1 CAMPING L'AVENUE VERTE
2, route de Villers Vermont
76220 Doudeauville
06 72 87 87 19
http://campingtipi.e-monsite.com
About 14 km (9 miles) from Forges-les-Eaux and about 11 km (7 miles) from Gournay-en-Bray. Some 3 km (2 miles) from the route at Haussez.

2 LA FERME LES PEUPLIERS
1542 Le Long Perrier
76220 Dampierre-en-Bray
02 35 90 22 90
www.lafermelespeupliers.com
About 8 km (5 miles) before Gournay-en-Bray

3 LA CAMPAGNARDE
936 chemin des Planques
76220 Dampierre-en-Bray
02 35 90 60 01
accueil-paysan.com
Single nights available at weekends

4 CHAMBRES D'HÔTES LA FERME DE WILLIAM
1235 rue Principale
76220 Dampierre-en-Bray
02 32 89 95 53   gites-normandie-76.com

5 CHAMBRES D'HÔTES "LA BRAYONNE"
167 chemin de la Vieuville
76220 Dampierre-en-Bray
02 35 90 10 99
chambresdhoteslabrayonne-bergerie.com
About 8 km (5 miles) before Gournay-en-Bray

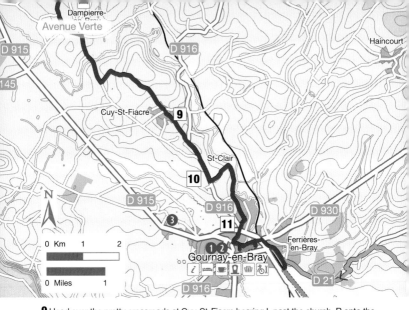

9 Head over the pretty crossroads at Cuy-St-Fiacre bearing L past the church. R onto the D916 to Gournay. This is one of the main roads into the town and can be busy, so you are advised to turn left to Cité St Clair.

10 L at the T-junction.

11 You will come to the signalled junction of the D916 with the N31 on the edge of the town centre. Proceed ahead on rue de l'Abreuvoir / rue des Bouchers to the town's main square. Markets are held here and on surrounding streets and there is the fine brick Kursaal cinema.

❶ HÔTEL LE CYGNE
20, rue Notre Dame
76220 Gournay-en-Bray
02 35 90 27 80 hotellecygne.fr

❷ HÔTEL DE NORMANDIE
21, place Nationale
76220 Gournay-en-Bray
02 35 90 01 08 www.hoteldenormandie.fr

❸ HÔTEL LE ST AUBIN
550, Chemin Vert
76220 Gournay-en-Bray
02 35 09 70 97 hotel-saintaubin.fr
A good km (0.6 miles) from the route

For more nearby accommodation around St. Germer-de-Fly see pages 78-79.

Kursaal cinema Gournay

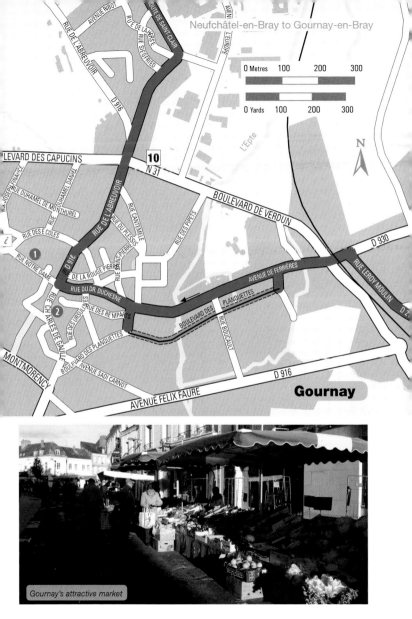

| 0 Metres | 100 | 200 | 300 |

| 0 Yards | 100 | 200 | 300 |

RUE DE LA VERSE
ROUTE DE SAINT-CLAIR
AVENUE NG01
RUE SIEGFRIED
RUE DE L'ABREUVOIR
D 916
AVENUE DE L'EUROPE
L'Epte

N

LEVARD DES CAPUCINS
N 31

10

RUE JOSEPHINE FINANCE
RUE DUHAMEL TANG
RUE DUHAMEL DE MONTHUREL
RUE DE L'ABREUVOIR
RUE DU PLESSIS
RUE CANTERELLE

BOULEVARD DE VERDUN

RUE DES PIPES
RUE DES E COLES
D 916
RUE SAINT-PIERRE
RUE DE LA ROUGE PIERRE
RUE NOTRE DAME

AVENUE DE FERRIÈRES

D 930

RUE LEROY MOULIN
D 2

RUE DU DR. DUCHESNE
RUE DES RE MPARTS
RUE DES URSULINES
RUE CH ARLES DE GAULLE
BOULEVARD DES PLANQUETTES
BOULEVARD DES PLANQUETTES
RUE BOUCAULT

MONTMORENCY
AVENUE SADI CARNOT
AVENUE FELIX FAURE

D 916

Gournay

Gournay's attractive market

Benedictine Abbey St-Germer-de-Fly

Gournay-en-Bray ~ The Vexin

Shortly after Gournay-en-Bray, St-Germer-de-Fly is important in route terms as it's here you must choose between western and eastern options (see overview map on inside cover). However, it's an attractive place in its own right, with an immaculately manicured centre and cluster of handy shops grouped around the magnificent facade of the wonderful medieval abbey. Heading down the peaceful lanes of the Epte valley you reach Gisors, dominated by its fine Norman castle which faces the 12th century church of Saint Gervais-St. Protais and is a hugely picturesque breaking off point before some wonderfully easy cycling along the high quality Epte Valley Greenway (*Voie Verte de la vallée de l'Epte*).

Route Info

Distance 60 kilometres / 37 miles

Terrain & Route Surface There are two climbs on minor roads, one shortly after leaving Gournay and another longer one leaving St-Germer and climbing above the Epte valley before a long road descent to Gisors. Once on the hard-surfaced traffic-free route out of Gisors both gradients and navigation are easy all the way to the gateway to the Vexin region at Bray-et-Lû. As on the route south of Dieppe, villages just off the traffic-free path are signed (there are no real villages directly on this route section).

Off-road 31.5% traffic-free on wide, smooth tarmac.

Profile

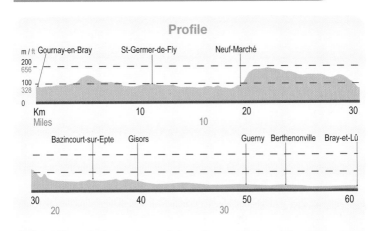

75

What to See & Do

• The highlight of tiny **St-Germer-de-Fly** is the Benedictine Abbey. It's hard to imagine a more peaceful scene today but it has a tortuous past; founded in the seventh century it was destroyed by the Normans, rebuilt in the twelfth century, and altered numerous times afterwards. The Chapel of the Virgin's stained glass copies Sainte-Chappelle in Paris. For cyclists it's the major route split on the Avenue Verte; head east for Beauvais and the Oise or south for Gisors and the Vexin.

• Sitting on the border of the Normandy and French Vexin areas, the town of **Gisors** was the focus of struggles between the Duchy of Normandy and the kingdom of France in medieval times. The castle stronghold overlooking the city, built in the eleventh century on a motte, according to legend housed the treasure of the Templars. It faces the equally impressive and imposing church of Saint Gervais-St. Protais, built in the twelfth century, which has the dimensions of a cathedral and a surprising mix of architectural styles.

Gisors castle

Church of St Gervais-St Protais

• The **Epte Valley Greenway** is a joy to cycle, a high-quality, well-surfaced route along an old railway line. Dotted with small villages and ridgetop castle remains, it parallels the clear and tranquil waters of the Epte river.

• Should you feel like carrying on south of Bray-et-Lû to the end of the traffic-free trail you will find yourself in the small attractive town of Gasny. From there you can carry on using minor roads to **Giverny**, something of an international tourist attraction, hordes flocking in coach loads to Monet's house and garden as well as the associated Museum of American Art. Monet's garden, complete with water-lily pond, is indeed spectacular. Also look out for Frederic Desessard's shop of miniatures and the historic Restaurant Baudy.

You can return to Bray-et-Lû by bike or carry on to the attractive working town of Vernon with its plethora of cafes, restaurants and hotels. If you want to shortcut to Paris by rail Vernon offers a direct 50 minute train service with selected services carrying bikes. Bray-et-Lû to Vernon is 18 km (11 miles).

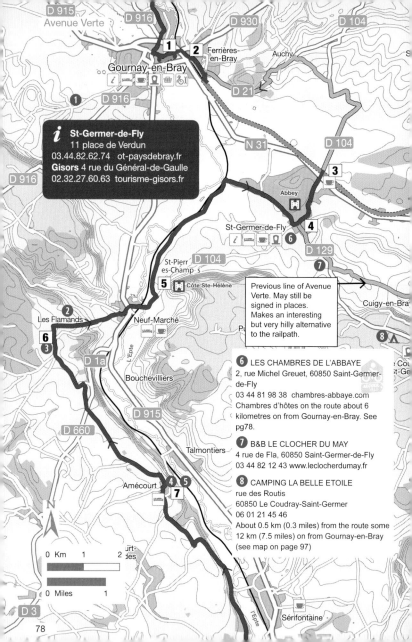

D 915
Avenue Verte
D 916
D 930
D 104

1
2 Ferrières-en-Bray
Auchy

Gournay-en-Bray

D 916

D 21

N 31
D 104

i **St-Germer-de-Fly**
11 place de Verdun
03.44.82.62.74 ot-paysdebray.fr
Gisors 4 rue du Général-de-Gaulle
02.32.27.60.63 tourisme-gisors.fr

D 916

D 104

3
Abbey

St-Germer-de-Fly
i **6**
4
D 129
7

St-Pierres-Champs **D 104**
5 Côte Ste-Hélène

Cuigy-en-Bra

Previous line of Avenue
Verte. May still be
signed in places.
Makes an interesting
but very hilly alternative
to the railpath.

2
Les Flamands

6
3
D 1a

Neuf-Marché

Bouchevilliers

8

D 915

6 LES CHAMBRES DE L'ABBAYE
2, rue Michel Greuet, 60850 Saint-Germer-
de-Fly
03 44 81 98 38 chambres-abbaye.com
Chambres d'hôtes on the route about 6
kilometres on from Gournay-en-Bray. See
pg78.

D 660

Talmontiers

7 B&B LE CLOCHER DU MAY
4 rue de Fla, 60850 Saint-Germer-de-Fly
03 44 82 12 43 www.leclocherdumay.fr

Amécourt
4 **5**
7

8 CAMPING LA BELLE ETOILE
rue des Routis
60850 Le Coudray-Saint-Germer
06 01 21 45 46
About 0.5 km (0.3 miles) from the route some
12 km (7.5 miles) on from Gournay-en-Bray
(see map on page 97)

N

0 Km   1   2
0 Miles   1

urt-
es

D 3

Sérifontaine

78

Directions

1 From Gournay's central Place Nationale bear L, onto Place Alain Carment, then pick up rue du Dr. Duchesne, heading east towards Ferrières. When the road becomes one-way east to west, take a R into a cul-de-sac. This is a no through road for motors but bikes turn L onto the delightful boulevard des Planquettes, a tree-lined avenue. This path crosses the Epte on a footbridge then rejoins rue du Dr. Duchesne by turning L and R. Beware – this section of the road is still one-way but bikes are allowed.

2 Continue to the traffic lights at a busy intersection with the N31. Cross the main road and the railway line then immediately R on the D21. After around 800m on this road turn R (if you pass the Danone factory you have gone too far), then R again. Just before the rail crossing pick up the lovely smooth traffic-free path on the L (actually part of the Trans-Oise route).

3 At the second road crossing you head R and take care crossing the main N31 / E46 onto the D129 to St-Germer and follow this into the lovely village centre.

4 At St-Germer's main square keep R for Neuf Marché on the D104 (the 'old' alternative route via Beauvais is still signed to the L- see chapter Gournay - Beauvais). At the next roundabout follow the Avenue Verte signs, leaving the D104. At a right hand bend split L up Rue de Boisville then L again before a railway level crossing. You will be rewarded with a beautiful ride on quiet lanes heading close to the railway and the river Epte that takes you straight through pretty little St-Pierre-es-Champs.

5 Just outside Neuf-Marché pick up the D104 once again and follow this for a short distance into the village, heading R just under the railway line, taking you past the lovely church to the traffic lights at the crossing of the busy D915. After crossing the main road take the L fork signed to Les Flamands and Rouge Mare, which becomes a long steady climb past meadows and a wooded ridge. Do look back before you reach the top for a wonderful view down to Neuf-Marché and the Epte valley.

6 Continue through Les Flamands, heading L then L again, onto the delightfully small C7, although you have the option of a short diversion of 500 metres if you continue towards the Rouge Mare memorial. This is a curious sculpture in a delightful woodland setting.

7 In Amécourt follow the road round to the R then turn L on the D660 out of the village, passing the tiny Chapelle Sainte-Anne. After a short distance fork L. At the next junction turn L and follow the road through woodland towards Sérifontaine. After Amécourt the road falls into the Epte valley, where it stays until Gisors.

Accommodation

1 B&B LE CHÂTEAU D'AVESNES
99 route de Gournay,
76220 Avesnes-en-Bray
06 07 66 81 53   chateaudavesnes.com

2 B&B LA ROSE TRÉMIÈRE
8 rue des Hayes, Les Flamands
76220 Neuf-Marché
06 03 89 11 86   la-rose-tremiere.com

3 B&B FERME DES SIMONS
21 rue de la Chasse, Rouge Mare 27150 Martagny
02 32 55 57 22

4 DOMAINE DU PATIS
1 place du patis
27140 Amécourt
02 32 55 51 51 / 06 89 54 09 01
domainedupatis.fr

5 CHÂTEAU D'AMÉCOURT
2 Rue du Buisson Bleu
27140 Amécourt
02 32 15 99 67
chateau-amecourt.com

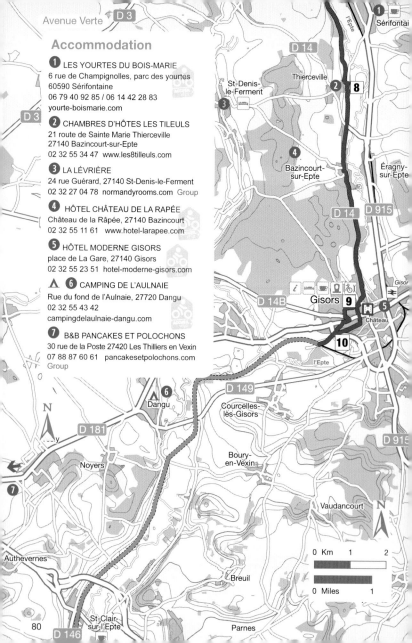

Accommodation

1 LES YOURTES DU BOIS-MARIE
6 rue de Champignolles, parc des yourtes
60590 Sérifontaine
06 79 40 92 85 / 06 14 42 28 83
yourte-boismarie.com

2 CHAMBRES D'HÔTES LES TILEULS
21 route de Sainte Marie Thierceville
27140 Bazincourt-sur-Epte
02 32 55 34 47   www.les8tilleuls.com

3 LA LÉVRIÈRE
24 rue Guérard, 27140 St-Denis-le-Ferment
02 32 27 04 78   normandyrooms.com Group

4 HÔTEL CHÂTEAU DE LA RAPÉE
Château de la Râpée, 27140 Bazincourt
02 32 55 11 61   www.hotel-larapee.com

5 HÔTEL MODERNE GISORS
place de La Gare, 27140 Gisors
02 32 55 23 51   hotel-moderne-gisors.com

6 CAMPING DE L'AULNAIE
Rue du fond de l'Aulnaie, 27720 Dangu
02 32 55 43 42
campingdelaulnaie-dangu.com

7 B&B PANCAKES ET POLOCHONS
30 rue de la Poste 27420 Les Thilliers en Vexin
07 88 87 60 61   pancakesetpolochons.com
Group

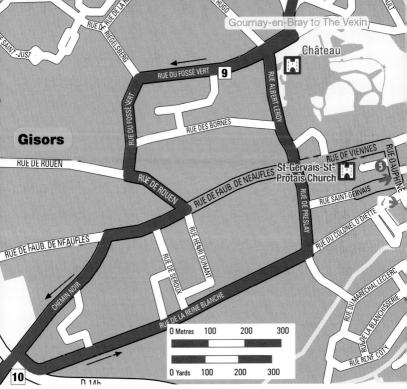

Near the bottom of the hill, don't be tempted to take the main road round to the L, but turn R up a gentle slope at the edge of the woodland. You may catch glimpses of the river Epte and a large château down in the valley.

8 In Thierceville turn R at a fine country house (actually B&B Les Tileuls). At the crossroads at the edge of Bazincourt continue straight ahead on the D14. In Bazincourt you will find a large number of fine old cottages and farm buildings. Carry on through the village and on towards Gisors, hugging the wooded edge of the Epte valley.

9 At the first major road junction in Gisors the official route heads R but we recommend you head straight over onto rue Albert Leroy which takes you past the classic Norman castle, which then offers fine views over the old town and the church and a good place for a picnic. For Gisors town centre head L on rue de Viennes and to head back to the Avenue Verte head back up rue de Viennes and over the lights onto rue de Faubourg de Neaufles. Look out for the L into chemin Noir,and you join what appears to be a country lane, back on the official Avenue Verte route.

10 Continue downhill splitting R or meet a roundabout. Head around it to cross the bypass and into the road opposite, which leads you to the "voie verte de la vallee de l'Epte" on the old railway line to Gasny on the R.

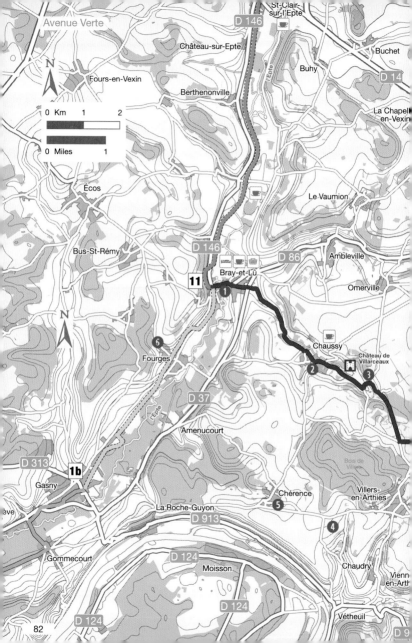

The Epte Valley greenway is a fairly new path and is not as well developed as the original Avenue Verte south of Dieppe. There are very few villages directly on the traffic-free path down the Epte valley, but at each road junction you will find a helpful sign to the nearest village, with an indication of the range of services available. The railway path is naturally very easy to follow and passes through woodland and open fields and is never far from the river Epte.

11 On the approach to Bray-et-Lû you will notice the old zinc factory, dominating the village. The railway path is cut by the road and a roundabout, where you need to turn back sharp L and immediately R into the village on the D86

1 B&B LES JARDINS D'EPICURE
16 grande rue, 95710 Bray-et-Lû
01 34 67 75 87
lesjardinsdepicure.com

2 AU RELAIS DE CHAUSSY
4 Grande Rue 95710 Chaussy
01 75 81 02 38 / 06 63 41 67 57
aurelaisdcchaussy.com

3 LA BERGERIE DE VILLARCEAUX
La Bergerie, 95710 Chaussy
01 34 67 08 80 bergerie-villarceaux.org Group

4 DOMAINE DE LA GOULÉE
17, route de la Goulée 95510 Villers-en-Arthies
09 61 51 80 49 / 06 25 99 81 47
www.ledomainedelagoulee.com
Sumptuous countryside b & b with swimming pool, sauna, fitness room and garden. Around 2 km (1.25 miles) from the route.

5 LA PETITE FERME
2 route des Crêtes 95510 Chérence
01 34 78 23 18
cherence-lapetiteferme.com

6 GÎTE DE GROUPE LE GÎTE DE FOURGES
c/o 27630 Vexin-sur-Epte
02 32 52 12 11 gitedefourges@orange.fr
fourges.a3w.fr / vexin-sur-epte.fr Group

Gisors is the only train station on or near the route and is the terminus of a direct line to Paris St-Lazare, 1 hour 30 mins away.
Transilien services, linking Paris to its surroundings, accept bikes outside of rush hours. www.transilien.com

Bray-et-Lû to Vernon option
At Bray-et-Lû don't leave the greenway but continue on it until its end at Gasny.

1b Cross a grassy area and car park to emerge at the southern end of the shop-lined main street to jink R then L up rue de l'Industrie. Follow this quiet road out of Gasny to rue de Vernon and head L to cross the D5 onto rue de la Treille. In front of the church at St-Geneviève-de-Gasny go L onto rue de l'Eau. Coming into Gommecourt wiggle L and R, staying on the Grande Rue before picking up the D200 on the R, signed Limetz-Villez.

Fine tarmac along the Epte Valley voie verte

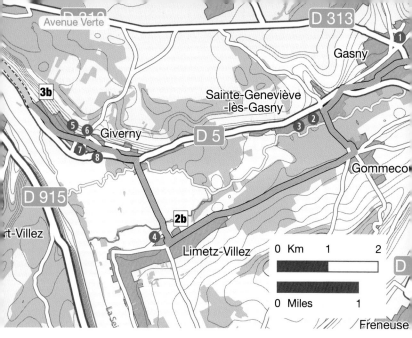

1 B&B LES AGAPANTHES
26 rue de Paris 27620 Gasny
02 77 74 12 62
bblesagapanthesgasnygiverny.com

2 CHAMBRES D'HÔTES LA ROSERAIE
2 rue des Jacobins 27620 Ste Geneviève-lès-Gasny
02 32 77 40 45
www.giverny.org/hotels/roseraie/roseraie.htm

3 CHAMBRES D'HÔTES AUX MARGUERITES
15 bis chemin des Jacobins
27620 Ste Geneviève-lès-Gasny
02 32 52 10 67   auxmarguerites.com

4 L'OREE DE GIVERNY - B&B
17, rue de l'eau, Limetz-Villez 78270
06 63 28 94 72
giverny-rent.fr

5 MAISON D'HÔTES LA DIME
2 rue de la Dime
27620 Giverny
06 20 83 28 90   www.ladimedegiverny.com

6 MAISON D'HÔTES LA RÉSERVE
Fond des Marettes
27620 Giverny
02 32 21 99 09   giverny-lareserve.com

7 LES JARDINS D'HÉLÈNE
12 rue Claude Monet
27620 Giverny
02 32 21 30 68   giverny-lesjardinsdhelene.com

8 HÔTEL LA MUSARDIÈRE
123 rue Claude Monet
27620 Giverny
02 32 21 03 18   www.lamusardiere.fr

9 BONS BAISERS DE GIVERNY
18 rue de la Ravine
27200 Vernon
06 64 91 71 29   www.normandie-tourisme.fr
Self-catering apartments.

10 HÔTEL NORMANDY
1 avenue Pierre Mendès-France
27200 Vernon
02 32 51 97 97   normandy-hotel.fr

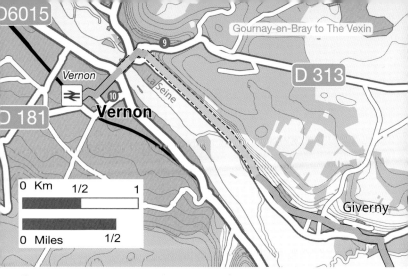

2b In Limetz-Villez, shortly after the handy bakers, head R onto the D201, signed Giverny and Vernon. Head up to the busy and fast D5 which you turn L onto only briefly, before heading R past the hotel La Musadière and through the village of Giverny, home to Monet's house and garden and the Museum of American Art. In season it's awash with tourists and associated gift shops and cafes and all but deserted out of season.

3b As you exit Giverney, just before the D5, head R onto the traffic-free trail. This ends at Vernonnet, where you follow signs to Vernon through backstreets then cross the bridge over the Seine into Vernon centre.

River Seine at Vernon

The château at Villarceaux
is on the Avenue Verte

The Vexin ~ St-Germain

At Bray-et-Lû you head onto small roads and farm tracks across the Vexin, designated a *Parc Naturel Régional* so as to protect its gentle landscapes, architecture and wildlife. The museum of the Vexin is housed in a lovely château at Théméricourt. Soon after the Vexin things turn a little surreal as just off the route, between Cergy-Pontoise and Vauréal, is the gargantuan sculpture cum landscape feature known as the *Axe Majeur*, a startling sight and well worth the short detour. Heading across the river Seine things become very grand indeed, fine châteaux at Maisons-Laffitte and St-Germain, punctuated by lovely traffic-free riding through the forest of St-Germain and alongside the Seine itself.

Route Info

Distance 60 kilometres / 37 miles

Terrain & Route Surface The route across the rolling farmland and woods of the Vexin is a succession of minor roads and farm tracks of varying quality, some quite rough. The area has little traffic; indeed it struggles with problems caused by depopulation. From Cergy to St-Germain there is a real mixture of surfaces as road sections link a whole series of tracks and cycle lanes, some tarmac, some forest track (as on your approach to Maisons-Laffitte) and some good quality track by the River Seine on your final approach to St-Germain.

Off-road 32 % off-road comprising all kinds of surface from rough track to smooth tarmac.

Profile

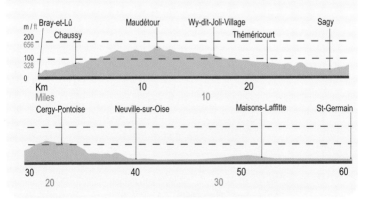

What to See & Do

• **The Vexin** is designated a Parc Naturel Régional with the aim of protecting its gentle landscapes, architecture and wildlife - as well as its human population who have been leaving the area steadily over the last few decades. You enter at Bray-et-Lû and head through the Parc Naturel's string of small, delightful villages using a mix of minor roads and tracks (dry weather only for the tracks at the time of writing - upgrading and new off-road routes were in the pipeline though).

The museum of the Vexin is housed in a lovely château at Théméricourt.
• **Villarceaux** is a beautiful country estate combining the ruins of a medieval fortified house, a sixteenth century mansion and an eighteenth century château set in sumptuous landscape gardens. The golf club restaurant is also open to the public and makes a classy lunch stop.
• The château at **Théméricourt** houses the museum of the French Vexin, showcasing its rare flora and fauna as well as local traditions.

© Creative Commons Pline

The pale stone of the Vexin, seen here at Théméricourt.

The surreal Axe Majeur at Cergy-Pontoise - just off the route but worth a visit

© Creative Commons Jean Pierre Dalbera

• Don't be tempted to keep pedalling past the modern surroundings of the Cergy area; it's home not only to a huge and attractive outdoor leisure park surrounding the ancient village of **Ham** but also the astonishingly grand **Axe Majeur walkway**. The walkway, just a short distance off the route, east of Cergy and Vauréal, is adorned with grand sculptures and in good weather opens up a lovely view to the area known as La Défense on the outskirts of Paris. It continues the grand avenue of viewpoints that crosses Paris, including the Arc de Triomphe and the Tuileries Gardens. The 3 km (2 mile) route starts at place des Colonnes Hubert Renaud at Cergy where the nearby bastide area and town clock are also worth a look.

• **Maisons-Laffitte** houses a grand château, acres of lovely forest tracks used for racehorse training and an attractive little town centre.

• **St-Germain** is altogether grander; not surprising as it was the summer residence of French kings from the 12th century onwards. The highlight of the current château is the terrace gardens, laid out by famous French landscape gardener Le Nôtre.

89

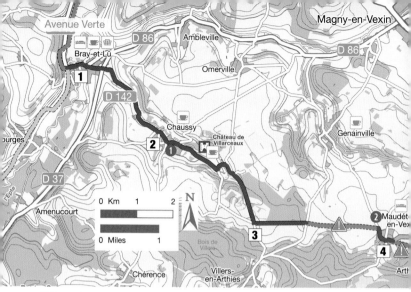

Directions

1 Having left the Epte Valley traffic-free path and headed through Bray-et-Lû centre go straight over a roundabout and start the steady climb out of the Epte valley. At the next junction continue straight ahead on the D142 to Chaussy and the Parc Naturel du Vexin.

2 You can't miss the church in Chaussy as it's built almost in the middle of the road! Continue up the valley to Villarceaux, where you catch glimpses of the château before it reveals itself. Turn L between golf club and château and climb steeply up the hill through woodland. At the top turn R then fork R towards Arthies, before descending gently. Continue uphill to a junction, now out of the Epte valley at a high point between Bray-et-Lû and Thémericourt.

3 Turn L at the crossroads with the D142 onto an unmarked road which runs straight as far as the eye can see. At the next junction the sign points ahead onto a rough track. This is not a mistake, it is the official route. It is passable on a road bike when dry, but likely to be difficult in the wet. Rejoin the road at Maudétour, where you turn R. Bend L then R to emerge at the church and here go L to pass the château on your right (a b&b).

4 The official route turns R down a stone track, but in wet weather you may well want to continue on the road to the north of this track, to Arthies.

Accommodation

❶ AU RELAIS DE CHAUSSY
4 Grande Rue 95710 Chaussy
01 75 81 02 38 / 06 63 41 67 57
aurelaisdechaussy.com

❷ CHÂTEAU DE MAUDÉTOUR
1 allée des Tilleuls 95420 Maudétour-en-Vexin
06 16 06 12 20 chateaudemaudetour.com

❸ CHAMBRES D'HÔTES LE PIGEONNIER
Château d'Hazeville 95420 Wy-dit-Joli-Village
01 34 67 06 17

❹ HOTEL LA CRESSONIÈRE
5 rue de la Cavee 95450 Seraincourt
01 39 29 42 61 hotel-lacressoniere.fr

5 Take the D159 to Wy-Dit-Joli-Village, which is a fast, gentle downhill stretch, crossing a roundabout in the process. Go straight ahead through the village, with a wiggle R and L. At the last junction in the village keep R and head out into open countryside. In Gadancourt go straight across the first junction and right at the second to leave along an arrow-straight, tree-lined road.

6 Another fast downhill leads to delightful Avernes, where you head straight across the Place du Marche. The official route takes us away from the village centre, with a L turn at the Grande Rue and a R fork up Clos du Prigent. Continue straight ahead until the tarmac runs out and join a rough track. Take a L then R on farm tracks and continue until you meet tarmac roads in Théméricourt.

You may prefer to take the D81 main road between Avergnes and Théméricourt to avoid these tracks, which can be muddy in wet weather. The Maison du Parc comprises an impressive château and an extensive public park. Not many facilities, but there is at least one restaurant.

7 From the Maison du Parc (north entrance) in Théméricourt follow the signs through narrow streets, turning R twice in quick succession onto rue d'Orleans, then left onto the D81 towards Vigny (rue du Pont du Bois).

i **Théméricourt** (Vexin) Maison du Parc 01.34.48.66.00
Maisons-Laffitte 41 avenue de Longueil 01.39.62.63.64
www.tourisme-maisonslaffitte.fr
Saint-Germain-en-Laye 38 rue au Pain 01.30.87.20.63
www.saintgermainenlaye-tourisme.fr

5 CHAMBRES D'HÔTES LE CLOS DU SAULE
2 Grande Rue 95450 Gouzangrez
01 30 27 94 99 www.leclosdusaule.com

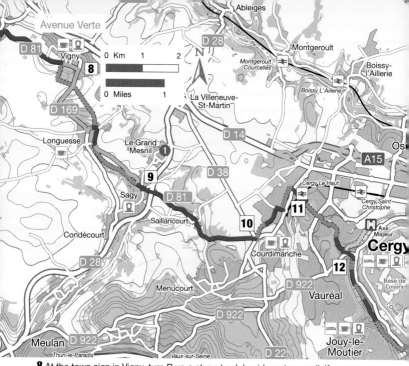

8 At the town sign in Vigny, turn R up a stone track beside a stone wall. If you are short of supplies you may want to continue into the town centre. Follow the track by the stone wall, cross a road (from the town centre) and continue onto another track, which climbs up and then down again into Longuesse. The surface is bumpy in places and you may prefer to take the D169 main road in the valley, especially in wet weather. Continue on-road then join another track, which has a compacted stone surface. Again there is a convenient on-road alternative nearby.

9 The village of Sagy is attractive with many old buildings. Pass the Mairie and R onto the D81 into the village centre with its artisan bakery and attractive looking auberge restaurant. L onto rue des Deux Granges. Take GREAT CARE crossing the trunk road out of Sagy, and head into Saillancourt. Through the village head L at a roundabout signed Sauf Riverains (residents only) to climb through trees.

10 At the roundabout bear L onto cycle track (signed V51). At the next t-junction turn L and join new cycle lanes on the road towards Cergy. Pass over two roundabouts then at traffic lights turn R and head L on a contra flow bus lane to arrive at the train station.

11 Turn R in front of the train station and follow the ramp down to cross a busy road into the park opposite. The narrow path continues under a road bridge, winding through an attractively landscaped park, passing under a small wooden bridge (beware path very narrow here). Head L on meeting a much larger tarmac path. Head downhill to join a quiet road (rue de Puiseux). Leave rue de Puiseux going R before the stone arch ahead and climb rue du Bardoulais under another arch to a busy road at traffic lights, heading straight over into the old town of Vauréal. Shortly Head R at a small T-junction.

12 Head across rue de l'Eglise with the old church to your L. Now continue on a varied high level route with views across the Oise valley. Simply continue on, with alternating sections of tiny road and unsealed track (including the lovely Chemin de la ligne railpath with its own little bridge). Shortly after Jouy-Le-Moutier (with its church and gardens down to your L) reach a road and head L downhill, splitting L and crossing a road to follow a pavement cycle lane towards the bridge over the Oise.

Note: For detailed mapping of the route around Cergy see pages 128-129

1 LE CHALET DES QUATRE VENTS
35 rue Narcisse Aussenard, 95450 Sagy
06 15 78 21 71
valdoise-tourisme.com Group

Cluster of reasonably-priced accommodation west of the route at Cergy, near Oise route split. See pages 128-129

See overleaf for the following accommodation:

2 LES CHÈNEVIS CHAMBRES D'HÔTES
3 Rue de l'Oise, Glatigny, 95280 Jouy-le-Moutier
09 71 34 73 24 / 06 13 13 15 13
les-chenevis.fr

3 HÔTEL LE CLEMENCEAU
1 rue Georges-Clemenceau
78700 Conflans-Sainte-Honorine
01 39 72 61 30 leclemenceau@yahoo.fr

4 HÔTEL AU PUR SANG
2 avenue de la Pelouse 78600 Maisons-Laffitte
01 39 62 03 21

5 HOTEL CERISE-PARIS
16 - 18 Rue de Paris, 78600 Maisons-Laffitte
01 39 62 11 91 / 06 95 18 61 66
cerise-hotels-residences.com

6 CHAMBRE D'HÔTE MSR HOFLEITNER
126 avenue du Général de Gaulle
78600 Maisons-Laffitte
01 39 62 86 49
https://sites.google.com/site/chezpatrickaparis/

7 CHAMBRES D'HÔTES LES COLOMBES
21, avenue Béranger, 78600 Maisons-Laffitte
01 39 62 82 48 / 06 71 13 61 06
chambresdhotes-lescolombes.fr

8 IBIS HOTEL MAISONS-LAFFITTE
2 rue de Paris, 78600 Maisons-Laffitte
01 39 12 20 20
ibis.com

9 COTÉ JARDIN
29 bis avenue Hortense Foubert
78500 Sartrouville
06 76 33 17 93
cotejardin-citybreak.com

10 HOTEL CAMPANILE
9 rue du Chant des Oiseaux,
78360 Montesson
01 30 71 63 34
campanile.com

11 CHAMBRES D'HÔTES LES CLÉMATITES
32 rue de Fourqueux 78100 St-Germain
06 82 80 73 05
chambredhoteclematite.com

▲ 12 CAMPINGS INTERNATIONAL DE MAISONS-LAFFITTE
1 rue Johnson 78600 Maisons-Laffitte
01 39 12 21 91 sandaya.co.uk

Numerous local Parisian trains (Transilien) and RER services (express trains), once you have crossed the Vexin, which has little if anything in the way of public transport: Cergy-le-Haut, Cergy-Préfecture, Neuville-Université, Conflans Fin d'Oise, Maisons-Laffitte, Sartrouville and St-Germain are all on RER line Ⓐ and the latter four are also served by Transilien trains.

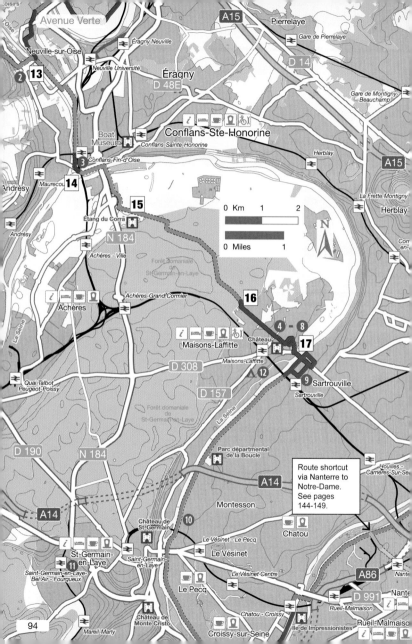

Avenue Verte

A15

Pierrelaye

Gare de Pierrelaye

Oise

Éragny Neuville

D 14

Neuville-sur-Oise

Neuville Université

Éragny

Gare de Montigny-
Beauchamp

2 13

D 48E

Boat
Museum

Conflans-Ste-Honorine

Conflans-Sainte-Honorine

Herblay

A15

3 Conflans-Fin-d'Oise

Herblay

Maurecou

14

La Frette Montigny

Andrésy

15

Corr
en-

Étang du Corra

N 184

Achères - Ville

Forêt Domaniale
St-Germain-en-Laye

Andrésy

Achères-Grand'Cormier

16

Achères

4 - 8

Château

Maisons-Laffitte

17

Maisons-Laffitte

Quai Talbot
Peugeot-Poissy

D 308

12

9 Sartrouville

D 157

Sartrouville

La Seine

Forêt domaniale
de St-Germain-en-Laye

Parc départemental
de la Boucle

D 190

N 184

Houilles -
Carrières-Sur-Se

A14

Route shortcut
via Nanterre to
Notre-Dame.
See pages
144-149.

Montesson

A14

Château de
St-Germain

10

Chatou

Le Vésinet - Le Pecq

St-Germain-
en-Laye

11

Saint-Germain-
en-Laye

Le Vésinet

A86

Saint-Germain-en-Laye-
Bel Air - Fourqueux

Le Vésinet Centre

Nant

Le Pecq

D 991

Chatou - Croissy

Rueil-Malmaison

94

Mareil-Marly

Château de
Monte Cristo

Croissy-sur-Seine

Île-des-Impressionistes

Rueil-Malmaiso

13 !Easy to miss! After crossing the bridge, turn right through a car park (the Beauvais loop joins from the opposite side of the road here) and join the riverside path Under the big road bridge go straight ahead onto a narrow bumpy track, which emerges onto a tarmac road beside the water works. Note route barred here at the time of writing; temporary deviation takes you L, on a rough earth path underneath the bridge itself then R onto a woodland path.

14 Beware lorry traffic as you approach Conflans-fin-d'Oise as it is a major port. Continue to the confluence of the major French rivers, the Oise and the Seine. At the railway bridge join the riverside path with large barges moored at the wharf. Pass under the road bridge and footbridge then sharp left and up the ramp to cross the Seine. If you want to explore pretty Conflans-Sainte-Honorine carry on by the quayside towards the imposing hillside square tower and church tower.

Over the bridge bear L onto avenue de St Germain, then shortly turn L between concrete blocks then R through a narrow gap into a housing estate. Wend your way on the road through the houses and just before the entrance gate turn right onto a cycle track. Follow signs for Maisons-Laffitte and Forêt de St Germain around a road interchange then turn L onto a crushed stone path alongside a stone wall, then turn R into the forest. Immediately through the wall over the metal animal grid, head across a small path.

15 Turn L at the first main junction you meet. Continue on the well surfaced forest track, across a crossroads, meeting a wooden post at a multi-way junction. Take the best surfaced track bearing across and R, signed route de la Vente Frileuse. At the road turn left alongside it, onto another compacted stone track. Follow this, leaving the road and skirting a military base on your L. Emerge through an old gateway into a housing area of Maisons-Laffitte.

16 Turn R onto the road, then left down the grand boulevard (avenue Albine) towards the magnificent château. Continue up to the château gates (the town centre is 2 minutes down to your R down the cycle lanes following avenue Ergle). At the chateau turn L down the side of it then R and R again at the main road. Follow to the roundabout on the north side of the bridge over the Seine.

17 Cross the river Seine on the main bridge leaving magnificent views of the château behind you. Take the first R into rue de la Constituante. Turn R again then L to join the riverside road. The tarmac gives way to a wide gravel path at the edge of Montesson, which you follow all the way to Le Pecq, where a new surface has been constructed through the built-up area. The majority of this improved section is alongside a quiet road, which can be comfortably used by cyclists.

Traffic-free, north of St-Germain

Beauvais cathedral

Gournay-en-Bray ~ Beauvais

The old railway linking Gournay and Beauvais has now been converted to a traffic-free trail. The old route is still signed in places though, the hilly ride making for some lovely panoramas across the rolling agricultural Bray countryside and the charms of the villages are low key and intimate; the characterful churches of Ons-en-Bray and Goincourt for example or the half-timbered buildings of the Bray countryside. There's also the usual very welcome accompaniment of a string of village bars and bakeries, providing ready fuel to climb the hills, somewhat lacking along the railpath route. Towards Beauvais the countryside changes, dominated by woods rather than farms, and on your final approach to the city you encounter the attractive Avelon and Thérain rivers. Cycle tracks and narrow back streets lead to the magnificent, dominating mass of the cathedral.

Route Info

Distance 39 kilometres / 24 miles

Terrain & Route Surface Plenty of hill-climbing on minor roads on perhaps the toughest section of the Avenue Verte, though a traffic-free link is planned for the near future. Remember the route splits at St-Germer-de-Fly between western and eastern options, this chapter covering the eastern option.

Off-road The lovely smooth tarmac of the Gournay to Beauvais railpath is now open and makes up 64% of the route.

Profile

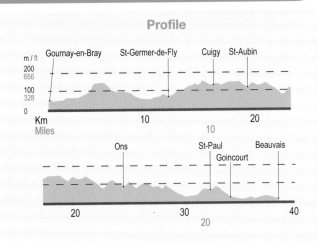

97

What to See & Do

- For details of **St-Germer-de-Fly** see page 76.
- A string of **attractive Brayon villages** line the route on minor roads between Gournay and Beauvais; Cuigy, St-Aubin, Ons and Goincourt all have their own unique, small scale charm.

A traffic-free route links Gournay, to Beauvais, but the old line of the road route was still largely signed at the time of writing and offers plenty of climbs, ridgetop rides and attractive views should you want more of a challenge.

- The chief attraction of **Beauvais** is without doubt its **cathedral;** intended to be the greatest piece of Gothic architecture in France it was never finished, suffering from grandiose ambitions that saw various parts being built only to collapse soon after. Even today it remains without a nave. Despite past misfortunes it still dwarfs the centre of Beauvais and houses a couple of fascinating clocks, one medieval that has continued working for some 700 years. The other is a masterpiece made in the 1860s, comprising some 90,000 mechanical parts. When the hour strikes, 68 automatons come to life and a magnificent clockwork display unfolds.

Beauvais cathedral

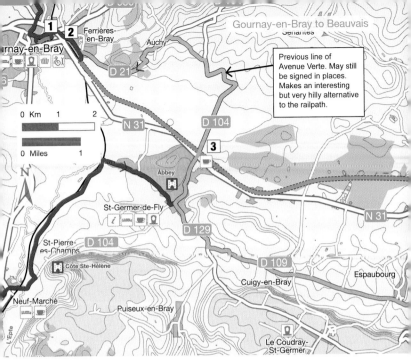

Previous line of
Avenue Verte. May still
be signed in places.
Makes an interesting
but very hilly alternative
to the railpath.

Directions

1 From Gournay's central Place Nationale bear L, onto Place Alain Carment, then pick up rue du Dr. Duchesne, heading east towards Ferrières. When the road becomes one-way east to west, take a right into a cul-de-sac. This is a no through road for motors but bikes turn L onto the delightful boulevard des Planquettes, a tree-lined avenue. This path crosses the Epte on a footbridge then rejoins rue du Dr. Duchesne by turning L and R. Beware – this section of the road is still one-way but bikes are allowed.

2 Continue to the traffic lights at a busy intersection with the N31. Cross the main road and the railway line then immediately R on the D21.
After about 800m on this road turn R (if you pass the Danone factory you have gone too far), then R again. Just before the rail crossing pick up the lovely smooth traffic-free path on the L (actually part of the Trans-Oise route).

3 At the second road crossing you head straight over for Beauvais, staying on the high-quality railpath (the road route up to the R is actually the western option to St-Germer-de-Fly).

4 Though not signed you can see some of the shops in Lachapelle-aux-Pots. The small centre has a pottery museum, a small lake (great picnic spot) and a bar and boulangerie.

5 Pass by the entrance to the fun park at St Paul.

6 Where trail ends go R onto the road (rue de Pentemont) and L onto rue du Faubourg St-Jean.

Note the route into Beauvais is reasonably well-signed but do keep your eyes peeled as with the busy street environment it is easy to pedal past the relatively small signs.

7 After just over a km on rue du Faubourg St-Jean turn L onto rue Tetard and cross the old railway once more then R, keeping on Rue Tetard.

Accommodation

❶ LES CHAMBRES DU CONFITURIER
18 rue de Gisors
60850 Lalandelle
06 18 37 35 82 / 03 44 82 64 38
chambres-confiturier.com

❷ LES CHAMBRES DE LA VALLÉE SURELLE
5 A rue de la vallée Surelle
La petite Landelle
60850 Lalandelle
06 33 69 48 37 / 03 44 48 89 83
chambres-lasurelle.fr

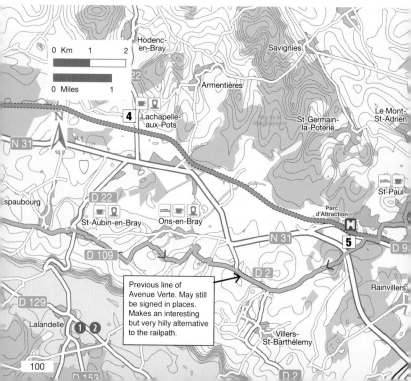

Previous line of Avenue Verte. May still be signed in places. Makes an interesting but very hilly alternative to the railpath.

Numerous cycle carrying
trains link Paris Nord station
to Beauvais taking around 1 hour 30
mins.
There are very infrequent bike carrying
services from Serqueux, on the
Neufchâtel-Gournay section, changing
at Abancourt, to Beauvais.

3 LA FERME GAUDISSART
1 rue du Marais 60000 Fouquenies
03 44 79 02 51 gaudissart.com
Hostel style accommodation for 15, some
4 km (2.5 miles) north of the route coming into
Beauvais

4 DOMAINE DU COLOMBIER
1, Grande Rue Route départementale 981
60155 Saint-Léger-en-Bray
03 44 47 67 17
www.domaineducolombier.com Group

Museum of the Oise, Beauvais

i **Gournay-en-Bray** 9 place
d'Armes 02.35.90.28.34
gournayenbray-tourisme.fr
Beauvais 1 rue Beauregard
03.44.15.30.30 visitbeauvais.fr

101

1 AU COEUR DE BEAUVAIS
3 rue Saint Paul 60000 Beauvais
06 45 18 48 19
aucoeurdebeauvais.fr

2 HÔTEL DE LA CATHÉDRALE
11-13 rue Chambiges 60000 Beauvais
03 44 04 10 22 hoteldelacathedrale.fr

3 HÔTEL DU CYGNE
24 rue Carnot 60000 Beauvais
03 44 48 68 40
hotelducygne-beauvais-picardie.com
Multiple rooms including a 5-person and a 7-person room. Storage for '15-20 bikes'.

4 SPQR DA MANUELA APARTHÔTEL
19-21 rue Gambetta 60000 Beauvais
03 44 05 90 08

5 HÔTEL CHENAL
63 boulevard du Général de Gaulle
60000 Beauvais
03 44 06 04 60
www.chenalhotel.fr

6 LA SALAMANDRE
10 rue Marcelle Geudelin 60000 Beauvais
06 14 87 59 53 lasalamandre-beauvais.fr

There is the usual collection of budget hotels near avenue John Fitzgerald Kennedy around 2 km (1.25 miles) south of the route as it leaves Beauvais, though they are hemmed in by very bike-unfriendly trunk roads.

8 Towards the end of rue Tetard turn L and cross the Avelon river on a footbridge (see town centre map opposite also). Now firmly in Beauvais, turn L to follow an attractive cycle track between the Thérian river and the boulevard. Cross the boulevard at rue du Docteur Gerard and turn L into rue Saint-Nicolas. Before reaching the church on the corner of a parking area, turn R into a narrow street with an attractive old timber frame building on the corner (rue du Tourne-Broche). Turn immediately L into rue de l'École du Chant, another narrow street which emerges onto a wider road with the magnificent cathedral to the right. Turn R onto rue Saint-Pierre and pass the cathedral into the city centre.

Beauvais's cathedral dominates the town
© Oise Tourisme

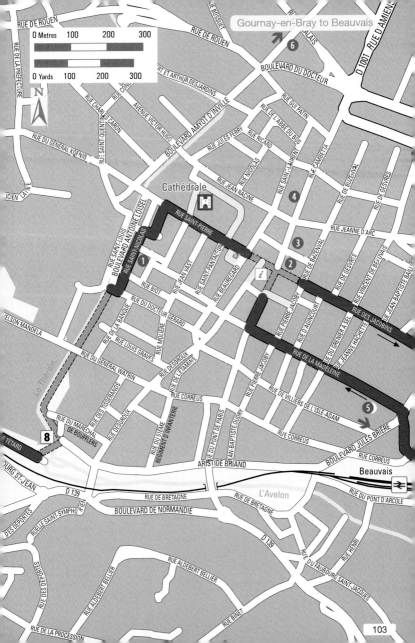

Cathédrale

Beauvais

L'Avelon

Le Thérain

The Avenue Verte
north of Senlis

Beauvais ~ Senlis

This section uses part of the developing ambitious cycle network of the Oise area, which will eventually total some 240 km (149 miles) of cycle network. This particular part links four of the Oise's most attractive and historic towns and cities; Beauvais, Clermont de l'Oise, Pont-Sainte-Maxence and Senlis via a succession of attractive small stone villages. Clermont has a lovely ancient centre and Pont-Sainte-Maxence a charming waterside setting but it's Senlis that has retained the most reminders of a rich past; as you wander around its cobbled streets and the graceful outline of its cathedral it's not hard to see why it was chosen as the backdrop to several celebrated French films.

Route Info

Distance 67 kilometres / 42 miles

Terrain & Route Surface Largely easygoing gradients with plenty of excellent traffic-free tarmac along the course of the Trans-Oise greenway, which the Avenue Verte uses here. The only real climbing comes, briefly, after Clermont and Pont-Sainte-Maxence. A wonderful traffic-free cycleway through the forest is used to approach the grandeur of Senlis.

Off-road 34% traffic-free, mainly on tarmac surfaces

Profile

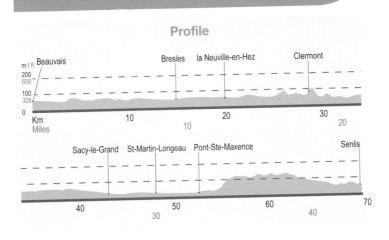

What to See & Do

• Pretty villages with pretty churches such as Bresles and Agnetz herald your arrival in lovely **Clermont-de-l'Oise**. In a pretty hill top setting (Clermont actually means clear mountain) you'll find the ruins of a twelfth-century tower, the Nointel gateway, the church of Saint-Samson and the chapel of Lardières.

• After passing through the Sacy marshlands comes your first sight of the river Oise at **Pont-Sainte-Maxence**. There's a relaxing marina and a flamboyantly styled church overlooking an attractive town centre. Nearby and en-route is **Moncel Abbey**, with sprawling grounds. More detail at www.abbayedumoncel.fr

Easy cycling on the Trans-Oise traffic-free trail leaving Bresles

Senlis

• The royal city of **Senlis** is a wonderfully picturesque end to the day's riding and a former haunt of French kings. Its timeless atmosphere is largely thanks to its ancient, encircling walls and the central and very graceful Notre-Dame cathedral combined with a patchwork of squares and alleys, peppered with monuments and mansions. With this rich architectural backdrop it's not surprising French films *Peau d'Âne* and *La Reine Margot* were shot here.

The town claims an unusual collection of museums too; art and archaeology, history and architecture (Hôtel de Vermandois), North African military history (Spahi museum) and the art of hunting.

Directions

For Beauvais detail see page 103.

1 In the city centre,continue ahead on Rue des Jacobins. At the busy T-junction cross the road and turn R onto the cycle track. Follow the signed route to the train station and bear L in front of it to follow a cycle lane through a retail park. The route joins rue du Wage, through a commercial area. Shortly after passing under a road bridge look for rue Matheas on the R. Follow the bend to the left, then turn right and cross another road into rue des Aulnaies. This street leads to an attractive woodland path, which emerges into a residential area. Head past the church and pretty half-timbered houses, bending L up rue de Sans Terre. R onto rue de Wagicourt.

2 At Wagicourt pick up the wide cycle lane on the opposite side of the road - now signed as the Trans-Oise route heading towards Therdonne.

3 Continue through Therdonne and turn L at a roundabout to join a cycle track, part of the ambitious Trans'Oise network. The purpose built cycle track continues by the D931 to Bresles' outskirts, a small town with an impressive church and castle.

4 At Bresles go R onto rue du Général De Gaulle and L past the very impressive town hall and church. Head R onto the D931 then L onto rue Grault to bring you to the superbly smooth tarmac of a traffic-free railway path. Just before the end of the path turn R and pick up avenue de la Gare to Neuville-en-Hez.

5 By Bar du Chene here wiggle L then R to pass the church and war memorial. Rejoin the impressive cycle track beside the main road. The route passes through a forest.

6 After leaving the forest, turn R onto rue Muids then L onto rue Robert Weiss into the attractive old village of Agnetz. After climbing to the church head R onto rue de Faye. Heading towards Clermont you see the impressive hilltop church and Nointel gateway.

7 Follow the one-way system through the town – at a T-junction turn L, then R and R again into rue de la Croix Picard, which climbs steadily to the attractive town centre. Turn sharp L into rue de la République, with the historic main street and church straight ahead up the hill. Turn R into rue du Chatelier below the church, then R and downhill into rue Marcel Duchemin.

8 Under the rail bridge bear R onto rue des Sources and after passing under a main road go R to climb to a junction and L into Breuil-le-Vert, where you turn L at a cross-roads. Turn R to cross the river La Brèche with its marshy woodland and continue to the village of Breuil-le-Sec. Bear R in Breuil-le-Sec.

9 In Nointel R at the end of rue des Boues and L onto rue des Courcelles to head out of town.

10 In Catenoy bear L and R to pick up rue des Courcelles again, and wiggle R then L shortly onto place de la Mairie, leaving Catenoy on rue de Sacy-le-Grand.

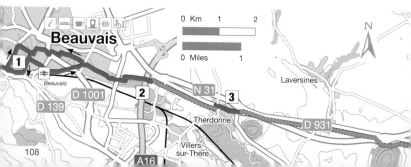

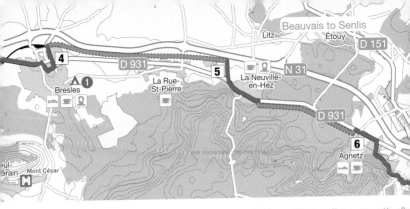

Accommodation

⛺ ❶ CAMPING DE LA TRYE
rue de Trye 60510 Bresles
03 44 07 80 95
www.camping-de-la-trye.com

❷ HÔTEL AKENA EXPRESS
156 rue des Buttes 60600 Agnetz
03 44 50 69 59 www.hotels-akena.com

❸ LE CLERMOTEL
60 rue des Buttes, Zone Hôtelière
60600 Agnetz
03 44 50 09 90 www.clermotel.fr

There are Paris Nord, bike carrying train links to Clermont (45 mins) and Pont-Sainte-Maxence (40 mins)

11

Catenoy

Avenue Verte

D 137

Labruyère

Sacy-le-Grand

12

D 10

Grandfresnoy

Sacy-le-Petit

D 1017

St-Martin-Longueau

D 13

Bazicourt

Houdanco

Verderor

N

N

Cinqueux

D 200

Les Ageux

Pont-Sainte-Maxence

D 200

L'Oise

Pont-Ste-Maxence

Pontpoint

Brenouille

D 29

L'Oise

Rieux

D 200

D 120

13

Abbaye Royale du Moncel

4

i Clermont 19 place de l'Hôtel de Ville
03.44.50.40.25
Pont-Sainte-Maxence 18 Rue Louis Boilet
03.44.72.35.90
www.pontsaintemaxence-tourisme.fr
Senlis place du Parvis Notre Dame 03.44.53.06.40
www.senlis-tourisme.fr

D 120

Mont-la-Ville

Fleurines

Mont Pagnotte

14

Villers-St-Frambourg

D 1017

D 932a

D 1330

15

110

D 1330

Chamant

A1

Scale:
0 Km 1 2
0 Miles 1

11 R onto the D10, a fairly busy and uninspiring road through agricultural land.

12 Pass through Sacy-le-Grand onto a straight run into St-Martin-Longeau, where the route turns right into the D1017. Join the slightly rough cycle track beside the road, downhill to Les Ageux and the river Oise. Major works were taking place along the roadside here in 2016, making cycling tricky, especially at the major roundabouts you pass over. Eventually meet the bridge with its distinctive curve at Pont-Ste-Maxence.

13 Immediately over the bridge L at the roundabout then first R into a small shop-packed pedestrian area. Shortly head L onto rue Henri Bodchon, joining the D123 and passing Moncel Abbey coming into Pontpoint. Turn R by the restaurant, bakery and bar and climb past the church of St Gervais into the extensive and beautiful Forêt d'Halatte. In the forest pick up Trans-Oise signs again.

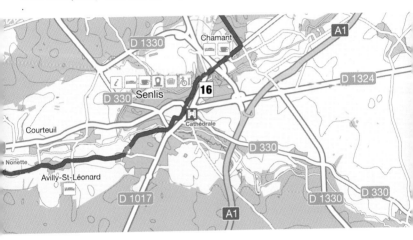

14 Head across at a crossroads to follow a traffic free tarmac track for several kilometres through the forest, a wonderfully isolated section. It becomes the route de la Chaussée de la Forêt de Pontpoint then straight across variously named 'Carrefours'.

15 After emerging from the forest, turn left into the village of Chamant and right onto the busy D932A. Cross over the D1330 dual carriageway and continue straight ahead at the lights onto the much quieter rue du Moulin Saint-Rieul.

16 Descend and keep L on Moulin Saint-Rieul. At the bridge over the river bear left into rue Carnot into the heart of this attractive medieval town with narrow streets and old stone buildings (see map overleaf). Cross a footbridge and small park with statue, continuing into rue St Pierre, rue St Hilaire and place de la Halle to the old town with attractive streets and numerous shops and restaurants.

Avenue Verte

0 Metres 100 200 300

0 Yards 100 200 300

N

RUE DU MOULIN SAINT-TRON

RUE DU MOULIN SAINT-TRON

RUE DU CLOS DE LA SANTÉ

ALLÉE DES MARRONNIERS

RUE DU MOULIN SAINT

RUE YVES CARLIER

RUE DU MOULIN DU GUE DE PONT

RUE DU MOULIN SAINT-RIEUL

AVE DU MARE

ALLÉE DES SOUPIRS

D 924

RUE THOMAS COUTURE

COURS THORÉ-MONTMORENCY

RUE YVES CARLIER

BOULEVARD PASTEUR

RUE DU CHAT HARET

RUE THOMAS COUTURE

AVENUE DE CREIL

RUE DE VILLEVERT

RUE DES FLAGEARDS

RUE SAINT-PIERRE

i

AVENUE DE CHANTILLY

RUE DU PUITS TIPHAINE

RUE DE LA POULAILLERIE

Cathédrale

AVE

RUE SAINT-HILAIRE

D 924

RUE DU CHÂTEL

1

GÉNÉRAL LECLERC

5

RUE DE BEAUVAIS

RUE LÉON FAUTRAT

2

RUE DE LA MONTAGNE ST-AIGLAN

3

RUE DE LA RÉPUBLIQUE

4

RUE BELLO

RUE DU HÉAUME

RUE DE BORDEAUX

RUE DE LA FONTAINE DES ARÈNES

RUE STE-GENEVIÈVE

RUE DES VIGNES

RUE SAINT-YVES A LA

BOULEVARD DES OTAGES

RUE VIEILLE DE PARIS

RUE DES CORDELIERS

RUE DE MEAUX

RUE DU LION

RUE DE LA POTERNE

D 1017

REMPART BELLEVUE

RUE DU QUEMIZET

La Nonette

IMPASSE SAINTE-MARGUE

RUE DE PARIS

RUE DE LA RÉPUBLIQUE

MIN D. LA POTERNE

Senlis

112

RUE DE L'...PÉE

RUE DES JARDINIERS

1 LA MAISON JULES
La Maison Jules 28 rue du chatel
60300 Senlis
07 87 99 92 94 lamaisonjules-senlis.fr

2 CHEZ SYLVAINE REERINK
3 rue de la Chancellerie 60300 Senlis
03 44 53 06 16 03 44 53 94 82
franceadom.fr

3 LE CASTEL ECOSSAIS
1 rue de Beauvais 60300 Senlis
06 72 08 26 80 www.castelecossais.fr

4 HOSTELLERIE DE LA PORTE BELLON
51 rue Bellon 60300 Senlis
03 44 53 03 05 portebellon.fr

5 LE PETIT BELLON
110 rue de la République 60300 Senlis
03 44 60 49 01 logishotels.com

There is a good stock of chain hotels on avenue
Général de Gaulle (to the north-east of the centre
off rue Maréchal de Foch) about
1.5 km (1 mile) from the town centre. Try Ibis
Budget Senlis 08 92 68 08 24, Ibis Senlis 03 44 53
70 50 or Hôtel Campanile Senlis 03 44 60 05 07.

Senlis' old town   © Creative Commons Alain Rouiller

Avenue Verte

An idyllic traffic-free approach to
Chantilly on the Avenue Verte

Senlis ~ L'Isle Adam

Heading back towards the river Oise from Senlis you get a glimpse of France's aristocratic history. Tracks lead through old hunting forests and the splendours of horse-racing Chantilly can't fail to impress, whether it's the moat-encircled château, the sumptuous horse stables or the surrounding lawned expanses that capture the imagination. An equally impressive reminder of the past is found in the beautiful cloisters and gardens of Royaumont Abbey. After skirting the charming town of Asnières-sur-Oise the eponymous river provides a charming backdrop to the final few kilometres riding into L'Isle Adam.

L'Isle Adam has plenty of services but is also a picturesque destination, with its own riverside beach and even a Chinese pavilion all waiting to be explored.

Route Info

Distance 37 kilometres / 23 miles

Terrain & Route Surface Easy gradients along intimate valleys and through woods on a variety of minor roads and tracks before some fine riverside riding along the Oise (though some sections may be a little rough).

Off-road 30% traffic-free on wide, smooth tarmac and rough tracks.

Profile

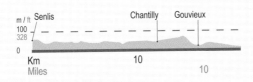

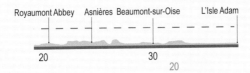

What to See & Do

• The charming Nonette valley and lovely traffic-free section of forest riding give you a chance to explore the grandeurs of **Chantilly**. Known as the Newmarket of France because of the racecourse and training stables here, it's a fascinating place to explore. Thoroughbreds can be seen exercising along the forest rides that surround the town and the two big races of the season, the Jockey Club and the Prix de Diane are incredibly popular.

The towering **17th century stables** are themselves a sight to behold but there are also acres of lawns around the town and its main draw, a fairytale-like **château** on its eastern edge, surrounded by a moat.

Art as well as architecture lovers might be tempted inside the château as it houses an incredible art collection. The library here also houses one of the most celebrated ever Books of Hours (a kind of 'primer' for devoted Christians of the time, with chosen prayers to be said at allotted times), this one being one of the most lavishly and painstakingly illustrated of all.

The Musée Vivant du Cheval is, as the name suggests, a museum with real live horses as the centrepiece and is housed in the huge stable blocks. There is a collection of worldwide breeds housed around a central ring where demonstrations of horsemanship are held.

Chantilly Château

Gouvieux © Creative Commons P Poschadel

• **Gouvieux** is a pleasant town most notable for its troglodyte dwellings that were largely occupied up until the 19th century then progressively abandoned (today a few are occupied, others used for wine storage)

• **Royaumont** is the largest Cistercian abbey in the Île-de-France (the area including Paris and its surroundings) and it is also a beautiful building in a lovely wetland and forest environment, its music season attracting worldwide attention. Access to the grounds and parts of the abbey 365 days a year with tearooms open weekends and public holidays. www.royaumont.com

• **L'Isle Adam** is a small-scale holiday resort on the river Oise, with two attractive wooded islands, one with a beach, 'constructed' around 1910 (currently open April-June weekends then daily until September) and originally conceived with slides, diving boards and waterfalls. Other things to see include a very reasonably priced local museum of art and history (Louis Senlecq), a wonderful and very old indoor market, and a Chinese Pavilion. There's also a lovely walk on the east side of the river Oise, across two small wooden bridges.

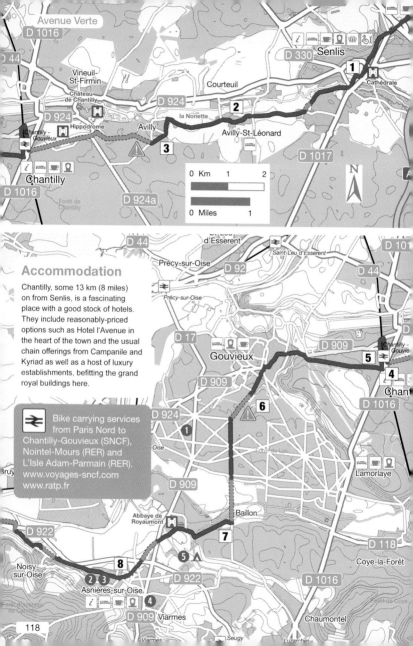

Accommodation

Chantilly, some 13 km (8 miles) on from Senlis, is a fascinating place with a good stock of hotels. They include reasonably-priced options such as Hotel l'Avenue in the heart of the town and the usual chain offerings from Campanile and Kyriad as well as a host of luxury establishments, befitting the grand royal buildings here.

Bike carrying services from Paris Nord to Chantilly-Gouvieux (SNCF), Nointel-Mours (RER) and L'Isle Adam-Parmain (RER).
www.voyages-sncf.com
www.ratp.fr

Directions

1 In the town centre turn L into rue Vieille de Paris by the town hall and head downhill and across the river. Turn R into rue du Quemizet past gardens and orchards. When the road bears left, join a track beside allotments. Rejoin the road and turn right into a pastoral landscape in the Nonette valley, a tributary of the Oise.

2 By the Mairie in Avilly-St-Leonard bear R.

3 In the village of Avilly turn L into the attractive main street rue du Calvaire. At the next junction bear R and at the next six-way junction bear R onto a wooded track, just before a road sign announcing your entry into the Foret de Chantilly. Bear L still on woodland track, following the fenced boundary of the Chantilly estate.

4 The track emerges into a car park outside the magnificent Chantilly château. Turn left at the château entrance up a cobbled road and at the roundabout turn right into woodland again. At the next roundabout stay on the road as it bears L and straight across the next roundabout, still in the woods.

5 At the main roundabout coming into Chantilly proper bear R and pass in front of Chantilly station. At the main road D909 turn L and pass under the railway bridge. There are two route options into Gouvieux, either use the cycle route beside the D909 or turn left after the bridge, then R onto the quieter chemin des Aigles.

6 Continue on the D909 through Gouvieux and where the main road bears R, continue ahead onto avenue de la République. This becomes a rough track through woodland, which emerges at a roundabout onto a private estate with limited signing. Bear L onto 9ème avenue. Continue through the wooded estate and join a gated road through open countryside, which leads to the village of Baillon.

7 At the far end of the village turn R, then R again to pass through an attractive parkland landscape with lakes and the Abbey of Royaumont. Cross the D909 onto a short stretch of old road, then cross the D922 into Asnières.

8 The route on Grande Rue skirts round Asnières' attractive old centre (worth a visit). Continue on the road towards Noisy-sur-Oise and on the outskirts turn R then immediately L onto the farm track, which leads to a bend on the river Oise and an attractive picnic area.

Accommodation

1 LE CÈDRE BLEU
20 Avenue de Précy
60260 Lamorlaye
06 68 11 31 72
chambres-hotes-foret-chantilly.fr

2 LE CLOS DES FÉES
42 bis Grande Rue
95270 Asnières sur Oise
09 52 59 83 65 / 06 07 56 47 32
www.chambreshotes-leclosdesfees.fr/en/

3 SWEET HOME CHAMBRES D'HÔTES
10 ruelle du Crocq
95270 Asnières sur Oise
06 85 32 02 50
sweethome-lacrouteetbuffet.fr

4 LA MONTCELLOISE CHAMBRES D'HÔTES
10, rue du Montcel
95270 Viarmes
01 30 35 36 62
lamontcelloise.pagesperso-orange.fr

5 CAMPING LES PRINCES
route des Princes
95270 Asnières-sur-Oise   01 30 35 40 92
www.lesprinces.fr
Camping and mobile home rental

9 After Noisy-sur-Oise the route rejoins the main road then bears R to pass under the D922, joining a rough track towards Beaumont-sur-Oise. Cross the busy D929 to enter town. Pass the bridge to the industrial area of Persan and leave town on rue Saint Roch.

10 At a large roundabout, bear L onto rue de la Cimenterie and through the small town of Mours. Once back into open countryside, the route leaves the road to the R and joins a rough track. Cyclists with narrow tyres may prefer to follow the D922 into L'Isle Adam. The track passes under the D922 through a subway, dropping back down to the river Oise.

11 Passing under two wide road bridges that cross the river, the route joins a woodland path set back from the river. This path can be muddy and slow going, but it soon emerges onto a road for a short distance. The route rejoins the delightful riverside path, passing fields and woodland. Passing a lock, the path continues alongside an access road and emerges onto the road adjacent to the attractive stone bridge, where the route turns R. A visit to the interesting old town of L'Isle Adam is well worthwhile, not least for the numerous shops and restaurants.

Bathing station at Beaumont-sur-Oise
© Creative Commons P Poschadel

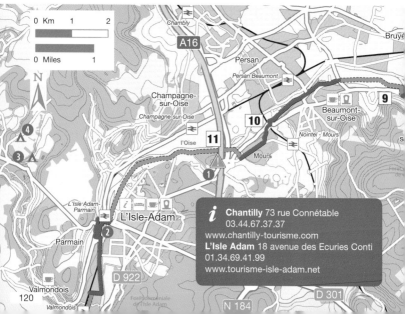

i **Chantilly** 73 rue Connétable
03.44.67.37.37
www.chantilly-tourisme.com
L'Isle Adam 18 avenue des Ecuries Conti
01.34.69.41.99
www.tourisme-isle-adam.net

1 HOTEL IBIS BUDGET
Centre commercial Le Grand Val
ZAC Pont aux Rayons,
95290 L'Isle-Adam
08 92 68 32 03
ibis.com

2 LE CABOUILLET
5 quai de l'Oise 95290 L'Isle-Adam, France
01 34 69 00 90 logishotels.com
Luxury option on an island in the river

There are several camping options a little
distance from L'Isle Adam:

3 CAMPING PARC DE SÉJOUR DE
L'ÉTANG
10 chemin des Belles Vues
Nesles-la-Vallée 95690 01 34 70 62 89

4 LE VAL DE NESLES VALPARIS
Chemin de la Garenne Rochefort
Nesles la Vallée 95690
01.34.70.63.24 levaldenesles.com

The Chinese Pavilion
in L'Isle Adam

© Creative Commons Cédric Quesseveur

The Avenue Verte at Conflans-Sainte-Honorine runs alongside the Seine

L'Isle Adam ~ St-Germain

From L'Isle Adam to St-Germain the Avenue Verte continues alongside the river Oise through an area that has inspired many famous French artists. After a fine riverside stretch the route takes to the main street of Auvers-sur-Oise, Vincent van Gogh's resting place, and not surprisingly something of a visitor magnet because of this. Another highpoint of this section is the town of Pontoise; like Senlis before it, it is full of picturesque old buildings and a favourite of film directors such as Roman Polanski. The route runs alongside the last stretch of the Oise before it reaches the Seine, having come more than 300 km (186 miles) from its source in Belgium. For the route from Neuville-sur-Oise to St-Germain see pages 94-95.

Route Info

Distance 41 kilometres / 25 miles

Terrain & Route Surface Riverside riding in the main, first alongside the Oise, then the Seine on a real mixture of roads and tracks, some traffic-free tarmac and some unsealed surfaces.

Off-road 36% traffic-free on a wide variety of surfaces.

Profile

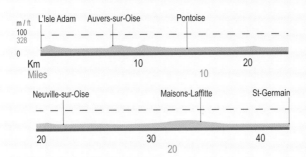

What to See & Do

• **Auvers-sur-Oise** was once home to Vincent Van Gogh and he and brother Theo are buried here. The 'Way of the Impressionists' walk follows the river and famous artists have signature paintings displayed at the spots they depict. Van Gogh only spent around seventy days here but painted more than seventy pictures. You can visit his room upstairs at Auberge Ravoux which is still a working restaurant.

Other artists also figure prominently in the town's history including Cézanne, Daubigny, Pissarro and Rousseau.

Daubigny's house is now both the town museum and home to a permanent collection of his paintings. Other buildings with strong links to the impressionist painters include the church and the house of Dr Gachet, Van Gogh's physician (open to the public).

© Philippe L PhotoGraphy

Auberge Ravoux, Auvers

Pontoise
© Joël Damase

• **Pontoise's** old town is built
on a limestone peak above the
Oise valley. Ancient squares and
cobbled streets lead to the 12th
century cathedral of Saint-Maclou
and what remains of the Carmel
monastery nearby. The town's
ancient ambience combined with an
astonishing network of cellars have
attracted filmmakers from Roman
Polanski to Olivier Dahan; it claims
to be the third most filmed town in
France.
• For details of **Ham, L'Axe Majeur,
Maisons-Laffitte** and **St-Germain**
see page 89.

Auvers
© Philippe L PhotoGraphy

Directions

1 The bridge crosses two channels of the river Oise into the town of Parmain. After crossing the railway line, there is a one-way system through the town. Heading south, continue past the station then turn L onto the D64 and D4. Turn L into rue de l'Abreuvoir, cross another road then drop steeply down to the river and pass under a railway bridge. Continue on the beautiful riverside avenue to the edge of the town and turn R, away from the river.

2 Just before reaching the railway, turn L onto a footpath that leads through to Valmondois station. Join a cycle track beside the road, pass under the railway bridge and follow another one-way system. Turn R into rue des Rayons, which runs close to the river but is separated from the water by private properties.

Auvers

© Philippe L PhotoGraphy

3 Turn R away from the river once more, cross the railway and the main road D4 and climb to join rue du Montcel. We are now in Auvers-sur-Oise, associated with Vincent van Gogh. The elevated street runs parallel to the D4 and passes several old buildings, with extensive views of the river. Continue on the old street past the church, Château d'Auvers and the Musée de l'Absinthe. Cross the D928 and rejoin the quiet road on the edge of the built-up area, with wooded slopes above.

4 The route eventually rejoins the D4, a busy but attractive road beside the river, with significant commercial traffic on the water. Pass the Pont de l'Oise, which gives the town of Pontoise its name, and pass under the railway bridge.

5 The route joins a gravel path through an attractive park beside the river. The path passes under the A15 autoroute and becomes rough and stony in places, before passing under another road and entering a pleasant agricultural landscape. The road follows the bend of the river.

Accommodation

1 GITE AUX ÉCURIES D'AUVERS SUR OISE
5 bis rue de Borgogne
95430 Auvers-sur-Oise
06 84 81 67 52 legiteauvers.com
Reasonably priced rooms in Auvers-sur-Oise

2 LA PETITE FUGUE
30 rue François Coppe 95430 Auvers-sur-Oise
06 82 99 03 88 http://lapetitefugue.canalblog.com

3 LA GLYCINE
8 rue Victor Hugo 95430 Auvers-sur-Oise
01 30 36 80 65 laglycine-dauvers.fr

4 LE GREEN DES IMPRESSIONNISTES
55 chemin de la Chapelle St Antoine
95300 Ennery
01 34 41 00 31 green-des-impressionnistes.com

A **5** CAMPING MUNICIPAL BELLERIVE
chemin de Bellerive 95430 Auvers-sur-Oise
01 34 48 05 22
Open from May to October

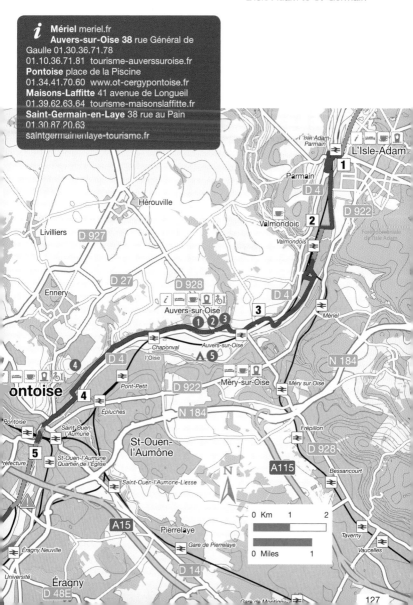

i **Mériel** meriel.fr
Auvers-sur-Oise 38 rue Général de Gaulle 01.30.36.71.78
01.10.36.71.81 tourisme-auverssuroise.fr
Pontoise place de la Piscine
01.34.41.70.60 www.ot-cergypontoise.fr
Maisons-Laffitte 41 avenue de Longueil
01.39.62.63.64 tourisme-maisonslaffitte.fr
Saint-Germain-en-Laye 38 rue au Pain
01.30.87.20.63
saintgermainenlaye-tourisme.fr

127

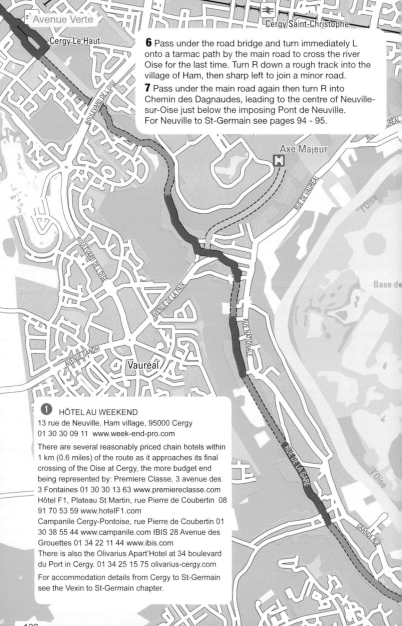

6 Pass under the road bridge and turn immediately L onto a tarmac path by the main road to cross the river Oise for the last time. Turn R down a rough track into the village of Ham, then sharp left to join a minor road.

7 Pass under the main road again then turn R into Chemin des Dagnaudes, leading to the centre of Neuville-sur-Oise just below the imposing Pont de Neuville. For Neuville to St-Germain see pages 94 - 95.

Avenue Verte

Cergy Le Haut

Cergy Saint-Christophe

BOULEVARD DE L'OISE

Axe Majeur

RUE DE VAURÉAL

l'Oise

Base de

BOULEVARD DE L'OISE

AVENUE DE LA PAIX

AVENUE GANDHI

Vauréal

RUE NATIONALE

RUE DE LA GARE

l'Oise

GRANDE RUE

❶ HÔTEL AU WEEKEND
13 rue de Neuville, Ham village, 95000 Cergy
01 30 30 09 11 www.week-end-pro.com

There are several reasonably priced chain hotels within 1 km (0.6 miles) of the route as it approaches its final crossing of the Oise at Cergy, the more budget end being represented by: Premiere Classe, 3 avenue des 3 Fontaines 01 30 30 13 63 www.premiereclasse.com Hôtel F1, Plateau St Martin, rue Pierre de Coubertin 08 91 70 53 59 www.hotelF1.com
Campanile Cergy-Pontoise, rue Pierre de Coubertin 01 30 38 55 44 www.campanile.com IBIS 28 Avenue des Grouettes 01 34 22 11 44 www.ibis.com
There is also the Olivarius Apart'Hotel at 34 boulevard du Port in Cergy. 01 34 25 15 75 olivarius-cergy.com

For accommodation details from Cergy to St-Germain see the Vexin to St-Germain chapter.

Cergy

BOULEVARD DE L'HAUTIL

0 Kilometres   0.5

0 Miles   0.5

N

6

DU PORT

BOIS

CHEMIN DES VOIES

1

RUE DE NEUVILLE

l'Oise

7

D203

l'Oise

CHEMIN DES DAGNAUDES

GRANDE RUE

Neuville-
sur-Oise

Neuville
Université

AVENUE DES SAULES BROUS

BOULEVARD CONDORCET

BOULEVARD SALVADOR ALLENDE

l'Oise

DE L'ANCIENNE GARE

A mixture of local Parisian trains
(Transilien) and RER services
(express trains) travel from the following
stations to central Paris: Valmondois,
Auvers-sur-Oise, Pontoise, Cergy-
Préfecture, Neuville-Université, Conflans
Fin d'Oise, Maisons-Laffitte, Sartrouville
and St-Germain.

Near the quai d'Orsay, Paris

St-Germain ~ Paris

Like London's own Thames, the river Seine is the heart and soul of Paris. Between the cultured attractions of St-Germain and Rueil-Malmaison the Avenue Verte passes through the idyllic landscapes captured by Impressionist painters such as Renoir and Monet. The scenery becomes even greener, virtually a countryside ride, along the Seineside *Promenade Bleue* between Rueil-Malmaison and Colombes. Waterside riding of a different kind, along the canals St-Denis and St-Martin, herald your arrival in Paris proper and journey's end at Notre Dame cathedral. Here on the Île de la Cité it crowns one of the most famous and beautiful views in the world at the very centre of one of the world's most beautiful cities.

Route Info

Distance 37 kilometres / 23 miles
Nanterre to Puteaux shortcut saves 5 miles on the above (pages 144 -149)

Terrain & Route Surface Largely following the river Seine, cycling into Paris along numerous easy, flat sections, is a pleasure. With many newly constructed cycle paths (though some of the route may still be under construction) you have what must be one of the most laid-back cycling approaches to one of the world's major cities.

Off-road 61% traffic-free on a mixture of tarmac and unsealed tracks, generally of a high quality

Profile

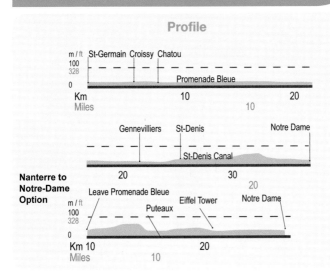

Nanterre to Notre-Dame Option

131

What to See & Do

• **Rueil-Malmaison** is an elegant suburb of Paris. It lies just to the south-east of the route, immediately after it crosses the Seine at the Pont de Chatou. The park of Bois Préau houses a grand château and there are fine walks and cycle rides along the east bank of the Seine and past the Île des Impressionnistes.

The town is strongly associated with Napoléon Bonaparte and his famous Empress Joséphine. The town walk in their honour links various buildings, such as the château bought by Joséphine with the money she expected him to bring back from his Egyptian campaign.

• **St-Denis** is a little way off the route after it has again crossed the Seine, this time over the Pont d'Île St-Denis, and is best known for its huge cathedral whose necropolis holds most of the tombs of French kings. The town was once a stronghold of the French communist party which drew its strength from the area of heavy industry that surrounded it. The area around the Stade-de-France (France's equivalent of Wembley) is currently being redeveloped and already houses 'Cinema City', a massive film production facility aiming to attract film making back to France.

Rueil-Malmaison

River Seine panorama, Paris

• **Paris's canals** may not be what the city is best known for but are a joy and a delight. Whilst the canal St-Denis is more functional transport artery than recreational facility, the canal Saint-Martin provides a glorious series of elegant locks, is lined with cycle lanes and on sunny weekends becomes a centre for those simply wanting to sit and enjoy their surroundings.

• The Avenue Verte's official end is at the world famous facade of **Notre Dame cathedral,** whilst at the other end of the Île-de-la-Cité are **Sainte-Chappelle,** remains of a splendid palace built by early Frankish kings, and the **Conciergerie,** where

Marie Antoinette and other leading opponents of the French Revolution were held before meeting their grisly end.

Once in the heart of Paris you can experience some of the world's most glamorous locations and some of its greatest museums easily on two wheels on the city's expanding cycle network. Whilst the **Louvre** and the **Eiffel Tower** top the list in the fame rankings there are a myriad of other delights here, especially around the River Seine and the canals, lined by ranks of stylish apartments and idyllic picnic spots such as the **parc de la Villette** and the **Tuileries gardens.**

133

Elegant houses en-route at Croissy

Directions

1 On leaving the urban area, the riverside path again reverts to a gravel surface up to the first of many large riverside properties in Croissy. One of the first properties is the British School of Paris. The riverside road here is very quiet, mainly serving residential properties. Note from Sartrouville until La Verrière tearooms by the riverside path at Croissy there are no shops or cafes to had – so make sure you are well supplied! The centre of Croissy is some distance from the river.

2 The riverside path / access road comes to an end at the railway bridge in Chatou, where you will find several shops. Pass under the bridge and join a cycle track beside the road for a short distance. The route crosses the Seine at Chatou and you need to turn L just before the bridge, up the slope and follow round to the R to join the cycle track on the south side of the bridge. Cross the river and take the zigzag ramp back down to the riverside. After a short distance on an access road, the path runs for several kilometres to Pont de Bezons with a good compacted stone surface. There is one water crossing, a substantial footbridge over the port access channel. There is a wheeling ramp beside the steps, but if you are heavily loaded you may prefer to use the lift.

Note: The Nanterre shortcut (to journey's end at Notre-Dame) heads R up boulevard du Général Leclerc around 600m after crossing this footbridge. See pgs 144-149 for more detail.

3 Between Pont de Bezons and Pont de Colombes the riverside path is well surfaced through a popular public park, but please note that the park closes at night.

Accommodation

1 APPART CITY
9 bis quai Conti
78430 Louveciennes
01 30 08 29 30 appartcity.com

2 CERISE HOTEL
2 rue Marconi
78400 Chatou
01 34 80 85 00 cerise-hotels-residences.com

© Creative Commons
Arnaud Camus
Château de Monte Cristo

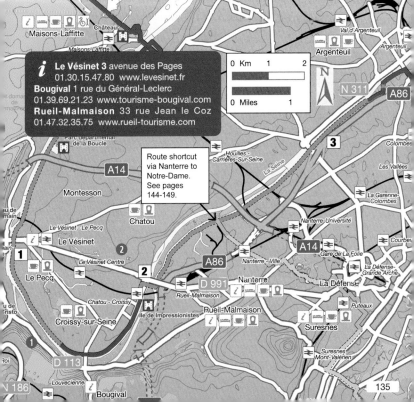

i **Le Vésinet 3** avenue des Pages
01.30.15.47.80 www.levesinet.fr
Bougival 1 rue du Général-Leclerc
01.39.69.21.23 www.tourisme-bougival.com
Rueil-Malmaison 33 rue Jean le Coz
01.47.32.35.75 www.rueil-tourisme.com

Route shortcut
via Nanterre to
Notre-Dame.
See pages
144-149.

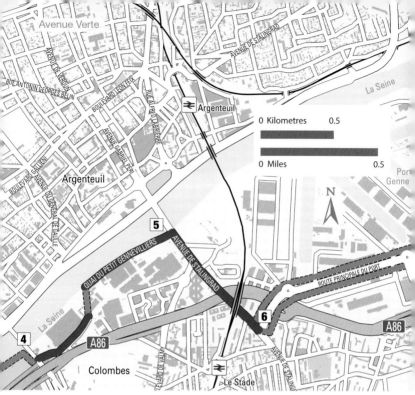

4 Head out of the park and at Pont Neuf (bridge) follow the path away from the river to cross the end of rue Paul Bert. Stay on the river side of the motorway flyover and use pedestrian crossings to access the footway beside an impressive brick building. At the end of this building leave the marked cycle track and turn L into an industrial access road. Just when you think you have taken a wrong turn, you will see a wide rough track between concrete walls. This looks uninviting, but it leads back to the riverside and a quiet road.

5 Cross the busy main road and turn R onto the shared footway. At the next traffic lights cross the road again and join cycle lanes on the road. Pass over the motorway and under the railway before turning L into the port access road.

6 This can be a busy junction and you may prefer to use the pedestrian crossing to access the cycle track in the middle of the road. The cycle track continues through the port area and you can get glimpses of the wharves on your L. The road bends gently round to the R and the cycle track comes to an end, turning into cycle lanes on the road. Head R at roundabouts.

7 R at this junstion, crossing over the motorway. Turn L at the large roundabout, where we recommend the use of the pedestrian/cycle crossings to join a two-way cycle track alongside the newly built tramway.

Lac des Chantereines next to
the route at Gennevilliers

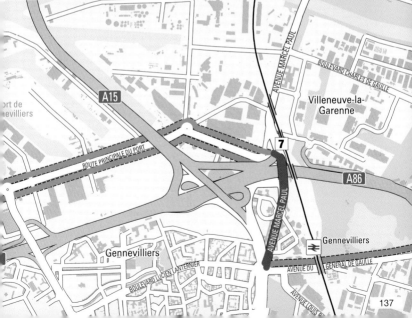

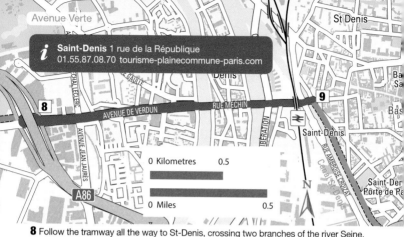

8 Follow the tramway all the way to St-Denis, crossing two branches of the river Seine.

9 Having passed under the railway bridge on rue du Port and crossed the canal, turn R and immediately split R again in the bus station area, to pick up the east bank of the Canal St-Denis. The towpath is very good where renovated, with a wide smooth concrete surface. At the locks cobbles have been retained, with a narrow concrete strip for bikes. Elsewhere, the surface is bumpy with the original cobbled wharves and railway tracks. This is a great way to enter the city, sailing under busy roads and railways along the way.

10 At Porte de la Villette you cross over the canal on avenue Corentin Cariou to join a

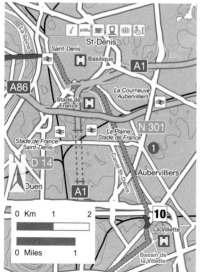

two-way cycle track on the west side of the canal. At the canal junction, continue round to the R, picking up the excellent segregated cycle lanes on quai de l'Oise.

Jink R then next L at rue de Crimée, onto more high quality cycle lanes along quai de la Seine.

11 At the end of this track turn L and go round the circular building. Cross over the busy road and under the elevated railway. Turn R onto rue de la Fayette and immediately get into the cycle lane in the middle of the road opposite and fork L at the lights for the cycle route beside the canal (quai de Valmy). Continue alongside the canal which bends round to the L.

12 Turn R into rue de Lucien Sampaix, which has a contraflow cycle lane (easy to miss). Straight ahead at a busy crossroads then ahead again onto rue Taylor.

13 Through the archway turn R onto narrow rue René Boulanger.

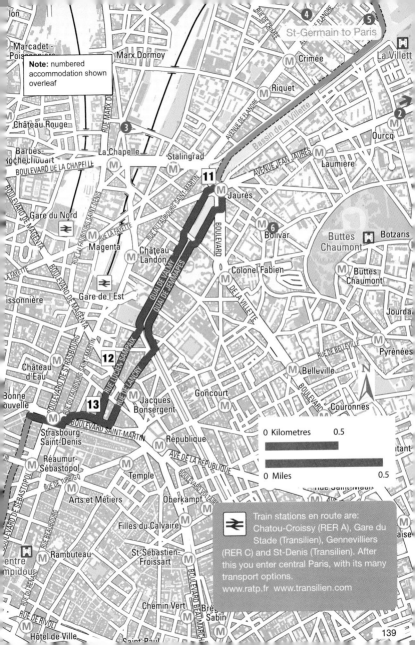

St-Germain to Paris

Note: numbered accommodation shown overleaf

Marcadet - Poissonniers

Marx Dormoy

Crimée

La Villett

Château Rouge

Riquet

Ourcq

Barbès-Rochechouart

La Chapelle

Stalingrad

Laumière

BOULEVARD DE LA CHAPELLE

AVENUE JEAN JAURÈS

Gare du Nord

Jaurès

Magenta

Bolivar

Buttes Chaumont

Botzaris

Château Landon

Buttes Chaumont

Gare de l'Est

Colonel Fabien

Jourda

Château d'Eau

Belleville

Pyrénées

Bonne Nouvelle

Jacques Bonsergent

Goncourt

Couronnes

Strasbourg-Saint-Denis

République

Réaumur-Sébastopol

Temple

itant

BOULEVARD SAINT-MARTIN

AVE DE LA RÉPUBLIQUE

Rue Saint-Maur

0 Kilometres	0.5

| 0 Miles | 0.5 |

Arts et Métiers

Oberkampf

Filles du Calvaire

aise

Rambuteau

St-Sébastien-Froissart

entre mpidou

Chemin Vert

Brée Sabin

Hôtel de Ville

Saint-Paul

Train stations en route are: Chatou-Croissy (RER A), Gare du Stade (Transilien), Gennevilliers (RER C) and St-Denis (Transilien). After this you enter central Paris, with its many transport options.
www.ratp.fr   www.transilien.com

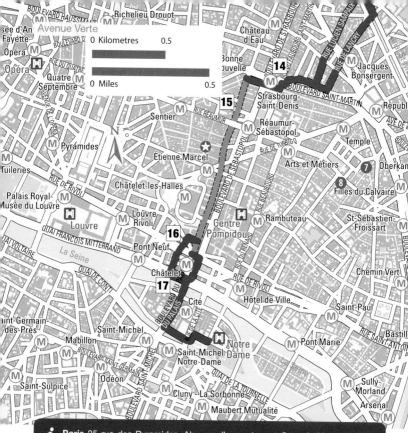

14 Great care is required at the impressive Porte St-Martin where you cross the main road and follow the cycle route markings first R into tiny rue Ste Apolline. Cross another main road and turn L into rue St-Denis and continue into the heart of the city.

15 This lower half of the street is pedestrianised and can get busy, but cycling is permitted at all times despite the crowds (see overleaf for larger scale map of end of route).

16 At the bottom end of rue Saint-Denis, just after crossing rue des Lombards, look for signs off to the R leading you down tiny rue Courtalon. At the end bear L, past an entrance to Châtelet Metro station. Head across rue des Halles onto rue des Lavandières Sainte Opportune to a signal crossing of the rue de Rivoli, going straight on. Continue straight ahead on rue Edouard Colonne, to a T-junction at the banks of the Seine.

17 TAKE CARE! Cross the busy road to turn L here. Next R to cross the river on Pont au Change. Continue straight ahead, along the bus lane, all the way to the next branch of the river. Don't cross it though, instead turn L for your final destination – Notre Dame de Paris.

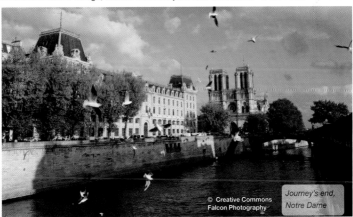

© Creative Commons
Falcon Photography

Journey's end, Notre Dame

See previous pages for accommodation locations ① to ⑥:

① ALTER ALIA
51 rue de la Commune de Paris
93300 Aubervilliers
01 43 52 29 69 alteralia.com
Hostel style accommodation with restaurant.
See map page 138

② AUBERGE CITÉ DES SCIENCES
1, rue Jean-Baptiste Clément
93310 Le Pré-Saint-Gervais, Paris
01 48 43 24 11 www.fuaj.org
Secure bike store.

③ AUBERGE YVES ROBERT
20 esplanade Nathalie Sarraute 75018 Paris
01 40 38 87 90 www.hifrance.org
New hostel with secure bike storage and bike hire.

🏕 PARIS CAMPSITES
There is one campsite within reach of central Paris, some 10 km (6 miles) from Notre Dame. Camping Paris Bois de Boulogne is west of the Bois de Boulogne (01 45 24 30 00) www.campingparis.fr

④ HÔTEL CAMPANILE LA VILLETTE
147 avenue de Flandre 75019 Paris
01 44 72 46 46
www.campanile-paris-19-la-villette.fr
Pricey (online discounts available). Secure undercover car park. Two minutes ride from the route at Porte de la Villette.

⑤ HÔTEL IBIS PARIS LA VILLETTE
31-35 quai de l'Oise 75019 Paris
01 40 38 58 01
ibis.com

⑥ RELAIS BERGSON
124 avenue Simon Bolivar 75019 Paris
01 42 08 31 17
en.hotelrelaisbergson.com See map page 137.

⑦ HÔTEL PICARD
26 rue de Picardie 75003 Paris
01 48 87 53 82 hotel-picard.hotelseal.info

⑧ HÔTEL JACQUES DE MOLAY
94 rue des Archives 75003 Paris
01 42 72 68 22 hotelmolay.fr

⭐ BLUE MARBLE TRAVEL
2, rue Dussoubs, 75002 Paris
01 42 36 02 34 Travel company that offers storage of bikes. See following site for detail:
http://bluemarble.org/ParisLuggage.html

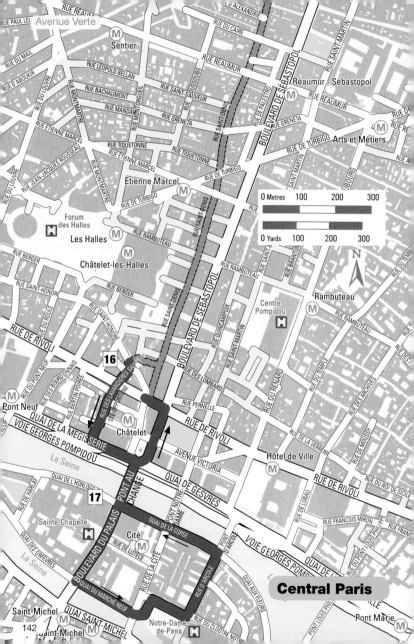

Central Paris

142

The lovely canal Saint-Martin accompanies you on the route into Paris

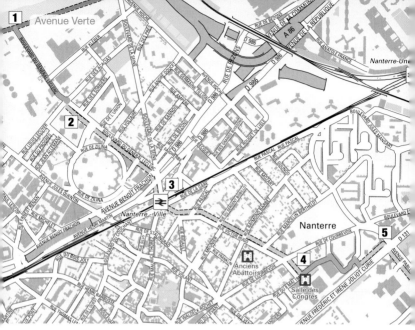

Nanterre - Puteaux shortcut

This shortcut shaves around 5 miles (8km) off the official route. It is unsigned but uses mainly cycle track and quieter roads - though be aware there are short busier road sections at Puteaux, briefly leaving the Bois de Boulogne and at the Trocadero. There is also some bus lane riding approaching the end of the route, so much younger / very inexperienced riders may prefer the longer and in many ways less scenic official route.

Directions

1 The Nanterre shortcut (to journey's end at Notre-Dame) heads R up boulevard du Général Leclerc around 600m after crossing this footbridge. See pgs 134-135. It is easy to miss; it is a small, unsigned cobbled street at right-angles to the official route which runs along the Seine and has a high wall on its L. Thereafter the navigation is rather easier.

2 Follow your nose along this road and at a mini-roundabout head straight across, picking up the pavement cycle lane on the R-hand side of Boulevard du Général Leclerc. Follow these all the way to a major junction, heading across onto narrow boulevard du Seine, which shortly brings you to the open area by Nanterre station.

3 Head for the station and use the subway under the lane, emerging to jink L and R by the little square de la Gare, picking up the excellent segregated cycle lanes on rue Rigaut. Follow the cycle lanes, splitting L onto rue Victor Hugo.

4 At the T-junction, behind Nanterre's very modern, pyramid-like town hall, turn L. At the roundabout R up allée Georges Politzer, bending L then R up this one-way street (you have a contraflow bike right of way). At the main road head L along the pavement cycle lane.

5 At the next main crossroads head R up avenue Pablo Picasso, to pick up the roadside segregated cycle lanes.

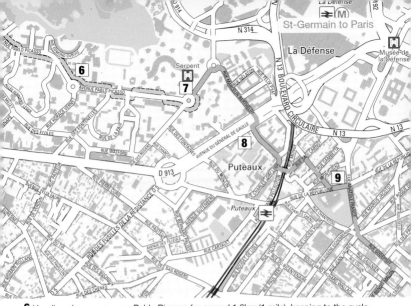

6 Heading along up avenue Pablo Picasso for around 1.6km (1 mile), keeping to the cycle lanes all the way, taking you over several roundabouts through this residential district.

7 Pass the striking blue, rounded tower blocks and the huge sculpture of a snake, heading L downhill to another roundabout and R uphill onto the bus lane on rue Marcelin Berthelot.

8 At the main road jink R then L onto rue Charles Lorilleux (contraflow bike lane), bending R before turning L onto rue Sadi-Carnot and immediate L over rail lines. Bend L and head R onto rue de Brazza, steeply downhill.

9 TAKE CARE! At the main road by the grand post office in Puteaux head L and immediate R, onto rue Anatole France alongside the pleasant green square. Pass the square to head across two sets of lights and onto rue Godefroy.

Snake sculpture, en route, Nanterre

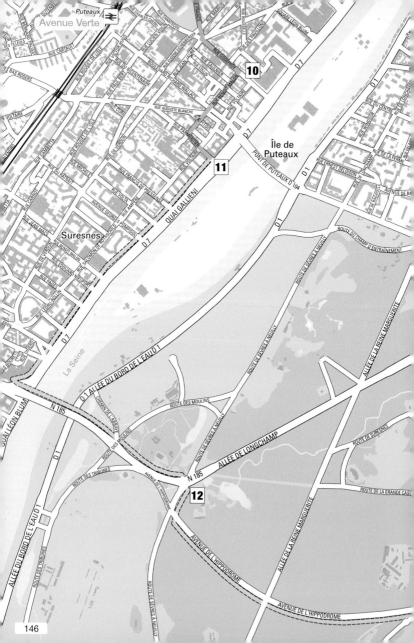

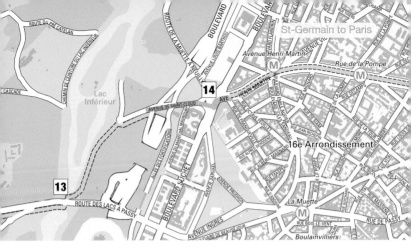

10 Take the second R off rue Godefroy onto rue Benoît Malon, and follow across one main crossroads to another crossroads with rue Parmentier and L, to emerge at the river Seine.

11 Turn R and use the cycle lanes all the way to the bridge, Pont de Suresnes. Stay on cycle lanes to cross the bridge.

12 At the second major junction head R across the road and pick up the cycle lane across that runs through the trees just to the east of the route de Sèvres à Neuilly. Meet l'avenue de l'Hippodrome and head L up the cycle lanes alongside it.

13 Around 1 mile (1.6km) after joining l'avenue de l'Hippodrome come to the area between two lakes (Lac Supérieur to the south and Lac Inférieur to the north). Head L up the western side of Lac Inférieur. Eventually bear R to pick up the cycle lane along avenue de Saint-Cloud.

14 The avenue de Saint Cloud brings you to a major junction at port de la Muette. Head straight across at this light-controlled junction, following the painted cycle signs on the road, then heading L and immediate R to pick up the segregated cycle lane along the middle of avenue Henri Martin. Cross a couple of major junctions as the cycle lanes continue up avenue Georges Mandel.

Lac Inférieur, Bois de Boulogne

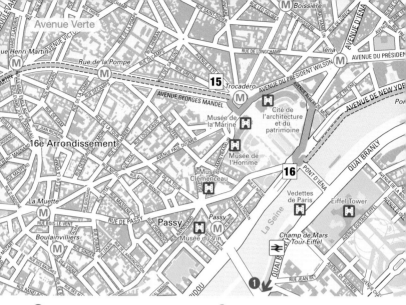

1 APARTHÔTEL ADAGIO
14 rue du Théatre 75015 Paris
01 45 71 88 88 adagio-city.com

2 HÔTEL BASILE
23 rue Godot de Mauroy 75009 Paris
01 42 65 99 54 hotelbasile.com

3 HÔTEL REGINA
2 Place des Pyramides, 75001 Paris
01 42 60 35 58 leshotelsbavarez.com
Sumptuous and very pricey luxury for finishing
treat. Well used to groups of cyclists.

15 Eventually come to the huge interchange of the Trocadero. TAKE CARE! Head around
the roundabout and just past the main entrance to the Palais de Chaillot turn R onto the
bus lane along avenue Président Wilson. First R onto avenue Albert de Mun and bear R at
the roundabout onto avenue des Nations Unies.

16 At the bottom of the hill TAKE GREAT CARE in heading across the road to the river and
picking up the pavement cycle lane on the L by the place de Varsovie, following the north
bank of the Seine in a westerly direction.
This rather narrow lane gives wonderful views across the river before the lane becomes
two-way after pont de l'Alma.

17 Shortly after heading past the Grand Palais over to the L, the cycle lanes end near the
pont de la Concorde and you simply stay on the north bank of the river along the bus lanes.
Pass the Tuileries garden and the pont Royal, keeping in the bus lane to pont au Change

18 Head right across pont au Change and follow the bus lane, all the way to the next
branch of the river. Don't cross it though, instead turn L for your final destination – Notre
Dame de Paris. (see map of central Paris on page 142 for more detail).

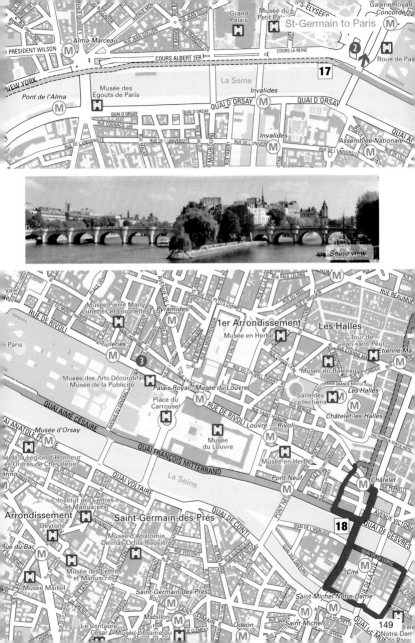

Galerie/Royale
Concorde
M

Grand Palais
Musée du Petit Palais

COURS LA REINE

Roue de Pa

2

17

NEW YORK

PRÉSIDENT WILSON
M

Alma-Marceau

AVENUE MON

FENILE GEORGES

RUE JEAN GOUJON

AVENUE DE FRANÇOIS 1ER

COURS ALBERT 1ER

Pont de l'Alma

Musée des Égouts de Paris

QUAI D'ORSAY

QUAI D'ORSAY

RUE COGNACQ-JAY

RUE DE L'UNIVERSITÉ

RUE DE L'UNIVERSITÉ

La Seine

Invalides

Invalides
M

QUAI D'ORSAY

M

Assemblée Nationale

RUE DE L'UNIVERSITÉ

RUE DE LILLE

Seine view

RUE PAUL LELONG

RUE DU MAIL

RUE BEAUMU

yale

RUE DE RIVOLI

RUE ST HONORÉ

Musée Pierre Marly Lunettes et Lorgnettes

Pyramides
M

1er Arrondissement

Musée en Herbe

Les Halles

Tour de Jean-sans-Peur

Étienne Ma

e Paris

Tuileries
M

3

Musée des Arts Décoratifs
Musée de la Publicité

Palais-Royal - Musée du Louvre
M

Place du Carrousel

RUE DE RIVOLI

Musée du Bateau

Salle des collections

Les Halles
M

Châtelet-les-Halles

SOUTERRAIN GRANDE BOUCLE NOTR

QUAI ANATOLE FR
M

Musée d'Orsay

QUAI AIME CÉSAIRE

de la Légion d'Honneur
es Ordres de Chevalerie

QUAI VOLTAIRE

QUAI FRANÇOIS MITTERRAND

Musée du Louvre

La Seine

Louvre - Rivoli
M

Musée en Herbe

Pont Neuf

Châtelet
M

RUE PERNELLE

RUE DE LILLE

Institut des Lettres et Manuscrits
M

Arrondissement

Saint-Germain-des-Prés

QUAI DE CONTI

18

AVENUE VICTORIA

QUAI DE GESVRES

Deyrolle

Musée d'Anatomie Delmas-Orfila-Rouvière

QUAI DE L'HORLOGE

Rue du Bac
M

Musée des Lettres et Manuscrits

RUE VISCONTI

RUE JACOB

Cité

Musée Maillol

Saint-Germain-des-Prés

BOULE

SAINT-GERMAIN

Mabillon
M

Odéon
M

Saint-Michel Notre-Dame
M

Saint-Michel
M

RUE SUGER

RUE DE LA HUCHETTE

QUAI

Le Centaure César

Musée-Librairie du Compagnonnage

RUE CLÉMENT

Notre-Dam
de Paris

irale

Organic cotton.
Unisex sizes XS–XL
£15.00

Avenue Verte
T-Shirt

Get the exclusive route t-shirt

shop.sustrans.org.uk

All sales directly benefit Sustrans' work and help to maintain
and develop the National Cycle Network

Sustrans is a registered charity no. 326550
(England and Wales) SCO39263 (Scotland).

sustrans

Where will you go next?

Check out more long-distance routes available from Sustrans

Pennine Cycleway North
Cycle Route Map

Pennine Cycleway South
Cycle Route Map

Land's End to John o'Groats
on the National Cycle Network

South Coast East
Cycle Route Map

South Coast West
Cycle Route Map

shop.sustrans.org.uk

sustrans